"Inspiring! Fascinating! ... w
God has used her to tou... a
must-read for all who have a heart for the lost and hurting.
Masterfully woven into this amazing story is Brindy's first-
hand account of how God used Natalie to reveal His great love
for her. The intersecting stories of Natalie and Brindy reveal in
both beautiful and painful ways the love God has for the least
of these. Read this book. Be challenged, be encouraged, and be
the difference for the forgotten ones."
- Stan Buckley,
Founder and Executive Director of But God Ministries

"Natalie's love for the Philippines and her journey through
falling in love with the street kids of Cagayan De Oro is a
testament to all followers of Christ. Watching her story unfold
and intertwine with Brindy's story has truly been inspiring.
This life-changing story is a must read!"
- Mayor John Henry Berry,
UPtv series "Small Town Big Mayor"

"An amazing story of faith, hope, and forgiveness, The
Forgotten Ones is a much-needed reminder that God actively
works on our behalf even in the midst of life's hardships and
emotional pains. Herrington and Epal have not only shared a
story, but a testimony, to how the Creator has a hope and a
planned future and purpose for every child's life."
- Jonathan Troll, Doctor of Psychology,
Child and Adolescent Therapist

"Natalie's heart and soul (and smile) shine through the pages
of this book, which is more diary than novel. We all have so
much to look forward to as we follow her faith-focused
journey."
- Lucy L. Scott,
SMU Broadcast Executive in Residence Emeritus

THE FORGOTTEN ONES

A Journey to Finding Freedom for
Orphans and Neglected Kids

Natalie Stephens Herrington
and
Brindy Epal
(contributing author)

The Forgotten Ones
A Journey to Finding Freedom for Orphans and Neglected Kids
Copyright © 2017 Natalie Stephens Herrington

MacKenzie Publishing
Halifax, Nova Scotia
August 2017
ISBN: 978-1-927529-47-8
ISBN-10: 1927529476

Editor – C.A. MacKenzie
Content Editor – Christine Rollings
Cover Designer – Mary Frances Stephens

ଽଡଔଓ
MacKenzie Publishing

DEDICATION

To the ones who feel forgotten and don't yet know they are loved... we're comin' for ya! You are not forgotten!

CONTENTS

PREFACE

"**S**ometimes, I wish I was no longer in this world... After losing my loved ones, I was filled with anger and loneliness. I'm suffering through normal life situations because of what I experienced. I hate my life. I hate being in this world."

The above are words of one of my dearest friends. Brindy is an orphan I met in the Philippines and unofficially adopted... Uncle Dick's Home was the first orphanage I visited in the Philippines. You will hear her story and mine intermittently throughout this book, learn how our lives came together, and what God did for each of us. I hope to inspire you to allow God to do the same in your life.

Throughout life, you've probably experienced tough situations—situations that shaped you into who you should become or who you are today. How many times have you heard the saying "I wouldn't change a thing!"? Most of us wouldn't. Once we've made it through a challenge, we may see why it happened or, at least, how we grew from it.

When you share your testimony—your story—with others, you don't omit difficult times, do you? That's exactly what makes your story incredible! That's what makes you *YOU!* Without what you've been through, would your story tell people who you truly are? My story doesn't reveal much about me without the good, the bad, the easy, and the tough...

When you think about orphans or neglected children, you may picture an orphanage, a community help center, or maybe adoption. What do you think it's like to grow up in an orphanage? What do the kids do every day? Do they go to school? Most importantly, how do they feel? Are they waiting for a family? Are only the lucky ones adopted? How do they feel when they are not adopted? Neglected, once again? How does the orphanage address that?

It's not about whether or not an orphan finds his "forever family" or "chosen family." It's about not having family and what that does to an individual psychologically, physically, emotionally, and spiritually. I believe adoption may help because a child is typically paired with someone who cares enough to help him or her to face what's inside—the emotional damage. Quite often, the focus seems to be on *those* orphans and how *they* cope. What about the rest? What about those who will never be adopted or cannot be adopted?

What comes to mind when you think of kids who never find another family? Maybe they grew up and continued with their lives, but I bet it wasn't easy and probably still isn't. In the process, they may have missed out on who they were created to become.

Family isn't the only answer to helping a child find his life, learn to love himself, and heal within. Odds are the majority will struggle with neglect, abandonment, loneliness, and self-worth. If a family isn't there to help, who is?

Two types of "forgotten ones" I refer to throughout this book are orphans and neglected kids; I reference neglected kids as "street kids."

A street kid is one who may or may not have a home, may or may not have parents, is most likely a victim of poverty, may have come from an abusive home, was or becomes neglected, may be addicted to drugs or alcohol, and lives on or spends most of his/her time on the street. Orphans have lost one or both parents and may live in an orphanage. Street kids are not always orphaned but are neglected and often forgotten.

My initial reaction to meeting orphans or street kids was to avoid making them feel different from me. As I got to know them better, I had the courage to ask what they had been through. Though it brought back the pain of their past, I realized they began to understand themselves better the more they opened up.

Why do we ignore the story of an orphan or, for that matter, any neglected child? Why do we ignore what they've been through? Maybe you're not ignoring it, but you may be avoiding talking with these children about their past in order to be protective. I have learned the hard way that that's not the best thing you can do. They need to get it out, face it, accept it, learn to use it for their good, and be able to live a full life.

The most protective and helpful thing you can do is talk about it and listen. That's what my journey has been about... I didn't ask until I had to for Brindy to let me in. I saw emotional struggles tearing her world apart, and it became a rescue mission.

I can't help all the "Brindys" in the world or even succeed by having them all adopted or cared for, but I can share my story of how God gave me a vision to make a profound difference and potentially change the lives of many children around the world. But I need your help. They need us to *hear* them. They need us to be there for them. Just as you and I need to interpret our own stories, they need someone to help interpret theirs by encouraging them not to remain silent. There is freedom in sharing. Will you listen?

The experiences I share pour the foundation for our organization, Ellipsis International, which we believe will address the forgotten or overlooked issues. All the stories in this book are true, but for safety and privacy purposes, many names have been changed.

"Ellipsis" is the grammatical term for the "..." used in or at the end of a sentence, symbolizing an unfinished thought or idea. We exist to assist orphans and neglected or abandoned children in defeating the odds by not allowing their situation to stigmatize their future. Instead, we enable them to finish their stories. We believe they have the ability to fulfill their purpose in life when given the chance. My journey and those I met along the way will reveal this forgotten area: to address a child's past experiences in order for him/her to experience freedom in the future by breaking the chains of bondage.

After you have explored the journey of *The Forgotten Ones*, I will share how Ellipsis plans to address these issues and, hopefully, free children from the bondage of their unavoidable pasts.

ACKNOWLEDGEMENTS

This book is a culmination of so many who believed in me, doubted me, and tested me (but also loved me) over the first twenty-nine years of my life. I couldn't possibly thank each person who has met me along this journey, but all of you have helped create this story, this journey, to freeing orphans and neglected kids. We are not done—we are far from it. But the journey has given me direction that is undoubtedly the Lord's path because He desires His children to break free from the bondage of their past through the power of the Gospel.

His love and your love have carried me.

It goes without saying that I couldn't have done this without my family. They have believed in me even when nothing made sense. This journey threw all of us for a loop but caused us to rely on the faith we have in Jesus. Thank you for standing by me and never giving up!

Thank you to the love of my life for allowing me to spend the last four years writing this. You have encouraged me beyond expectation. I truly couldn't imagine this journey without you. God will give us the desires of our heart to see freedom abound in children around the world! Let's do this!

Of course, I have to thank Jesus for choosing me to go on this journey. I am honored to be a part of His plan in allowing me to be His hands and feet.

And though I can't be grateful for what she has been through, I am honored to have stood by Brindy's side to help her face the giants in her past. Together, we found a way through the worst moments of her life so she could experience the joy of her salvation in the freedom of Jesus Christ. Thank you for trusting me.

INTRODUCTION

"What do you want to be when you grow up?" I asked.

Brindy looked at me, puzzled, and then stared at her blank piece of paper.

I scanned the bare, dim room, seeing only a few long tables covered in plastic tablecloths. A couple of posters from the previous Christmas hung on the bland walls. Mismatched curtains had been knotted to keep them from blowing with the wind when the wooden levers were open.

There wasn't much inspiration in the room, but outside those windows, despite rain dancing on the tin roof, was a tropical oasis. This was a haven. The children couldn't see it, but I saw hopes and dreams around the room. Beautiful brown faces smiled at me as if I had asked a silly question.

I looked back at Brindy to find her drawing flowers instead of answering the question. She seemed to be the only one who wasn't trying, but I knew she was pondering something. I asked her to work on the paper in her spare time.

I threw out ideas to help their creative juices flow: "Doctor, teacher, nurse..."

At the end of our session, I gathered the papers as they left the room. I had expected to read dream occupations—lawyer, policeman, or Superman. I was astonished at the number of answers that said, "I want to get a job so I can help my family one day!"

That moment moved me. *Why don't I think with such simplicity even now—much less at their age?* Dumbfounded, I went for a walk.

Away from the cafeteria, I heard girls giggling and balls bouncing as they played "Jack Stone," commonly referred to as Jacks but using stones instead of jacks.

Everything was a vibrant green since the rain had stopped, and I truly felt I could get lost in the jungle even though the orphanage property wasn't that vast. I walked to the edge of the property and stood by the fence, which provided a barrier from the enormous cliff and valley below. No matter how many times I'd walked to that point, I could never fully grasp its beauty: the shades of green and brown on the mountains across the river, the azure sky, the pale yellow and pink flowers, and the outline of coconut trees on the mountain peaks. This was where I came to think, dream, and pray. Ironically, this place helped me dream among children who seemed to struggle dreaming.

I pondered the kids' answers to what I thought was the easiest question for kids around the world. They didn't believe they could be whatever they wanted to be when they grew up, contrary to my American upbringing. In that moment, my heart sank. Where would I be if no one had ever encouraged or believed in me and assured me I was capable?

I cannot count the number of projects and assignments based around what kids want to be when they grew up, even assignments like "Bring Your Parent to School Day." In most third world countries, children are taught merely to survive—to make a living (it doesn't matter how) and provide for their extended family.

I decided then that I wanted one of my goals at the orphanage to be teaching these kids to believe in themselves. To do that, I needed to find a way to help them believe they could be anything they wanted to be.

The Forgotten Ones

*A Journey to Finding Freedom for
Orphans and Neglected Kids*

1

My heart ached as we drove away from Uncle Dick's Home, countless hands waving in my direction. I knew it wasn't over; I knew I'd be back. God placed a burden on my heart for this nation and *the forgotten ones* living there. There was much to be done.

Upon returning to Mississippi in December 2010 after three months in the Philippines, I felt lost. *What does one do after living in an orphanage in a third world country? How do I justify my bountiful American lifestyle after seeing people living with less?* My thoughts were all over the place, but God wasn't calling me to go back yet. This would be a season of learning, but I wasn't sure how...

Torn between going to seminary and finding a job, I sat around waiting for God to tell me what to choose. I was trusting the Lord but not working with what He had already revealed. At a Passion Conference in Atlanta, I attended the last message in which Louie Giglio shared, "It doesn't matter where you go or what you do as long as you take the name of Jesus with you!" At that moment, I realized God was pleased with either decision, and He was waiting for me to decide to trust Him by walking in faith.

Seminary seemed like the best thing to do, as it would train me for what God had in store for me next. Because I had waited around for God to speak from Heaven, I was too late to start on campus, so I signed up for online classes that January. I was living at home in Mississippi at the time and applied at Southwestern Baptist Theological Seminary in Ft. Worth, Texas.

In May of 2011, I moved to Dallas and took a two-week course. On the first day, I wandered aimlessly trying to find my class when I met Luis. We were headed in the same direction, so he asked if I was in his class. He showed me where we were meeting, and over the next few days, we talked. He worked at Prestonwood Baptist Church in Plano, Texas. I assumed it was a small country church and didn't think much about it.

At the time, I was searching for a part-time job in missions ministry or children's ministry. After our two-week course ended, Luis emailed me about a position, the Young Singles Women's Director, which had opened at Prestonwood. He said I'd be great at it and gave me the email of the person to contact in case I was interested. I had no desire to work in women's ministry because it didn't seem to fit with how God had changed my life the previous year, but I applied anyway.

The next day, I received a call from the Young Singles Minister, Matt, to come in for an interview. It was a pleasant surprise to find out he was from Mississippi as well. What a small world!

When I arrived, I was sure my GPS was broken and almost returned home. For a small-town girl, I had never seen anything like this. The church was huge. No way was *this* a church, and no way would *they* want *me* to work there! I quickly found out many people referred to it as "Six Flags Over Jesus." Prestonwood has over 30,000 members.

I was completely wrong about the size of the church, assuming it would be small. *There's no way I'm getting this job! I just started seminary, and I don't have any experience in women's ministry!*

I felt the Lord assuring me that this was part of His plan regardless of the outcome. I'd been recommended for the interview for a reason. If anything, interview practice was a good thing.

In the interview, God showed me all the ways He had prepared me for women's ministry—not through education but experience. I had been in a seven-year relationship and knew what young, single women struggled with: identity, dating, career, and the real world. I realized I had been through a lot, more than most women, so even though I was twenty-three, I could lead single women ranging from twenty-two to thirty-four in this ministry. After the interview, I knew everything was in the Lord's hands.

To my surprise, I got the job! It challenged me more than I had ever been challenged. I learned so much about leadership, both in my position as well as in ministry. God stretched me and taught me in that season. He put me in situations that seemed hopeless, but He gave me a way out and many found Jesus. The ministry taught me how to seek Him and brought me to my knees daily when I faced situations I wasn't qualified to handle. I saw how this season of learning was preparing me to return to the Philippines.

2

I define most of my life as full of misery. I hated the world. I hated everything after my parents passed away; I hated myself, and sometimes I hated God.

I came from a poor family. We lived in the mountains. My father was a corn farmer, and my mother was a housekeeper. I have three siblings.

One day, my mother asked if I wanted to go with her to the hospital because she had an appointment to have a mole removed from her left hand. The operation was successful, but a few days later, she was throwing up and had a high fever. She wouldn't eat. The next morning, my father took my mother back to the hospital. My siblings and I stayed home.

About 3 p.m., heavy rain and wind started. As a child, I loved playing in the rain with my siblings, and we were so happy then. It was the most fun we'd ever had! Shortly after the rain stopped at 5 p.m., a relative came to our house and said, "Your mother passed away."

We were all shocked. I was seven years old. I had no cares in the world nor did I understand what was happening. After thirty days, they buried my mother. I remember that day watching my brother try to go in the hole with my mom. Someone had to hold him back. My sister and I were crying as we watched my little brother, who was confused about what was happening to Mom.

After my mother died, our house was different. No one cleaned or cooked, and worst of all, no one took care of us, understood us, or loved us. Nothing was the same again.

3

I've always desired to adopt a child. At an early age, I pushed that desire away, knowing it was something for the future... After all, that's what many kids do. They dream of the future and, most of the time, never do anything about it. I was too young then anyway.

I grew up as the fifth generation of my family in Magee, Mississippi, a small town of 4,500 people, south of Jackson. Magee sits about halfway between Jackson and Hattiesburg, two of the larger metropolitan areas in Mississippi. Many people pass through Magee each day, going between the larger cities. There are two stoplights and a Walmart.

It felt like one big family growing up in Magee, a quaint place where family came first. With the warm weather and enough land to allow kids to expend their holiday excitement, it was a popular destination to host family holiday gatherings. There were many family-owned businesses, and Magee maintained its charm over the years. Everyone knew each other. Our family was known because my grandfather was one of the first doctors in town.

Nearby were three schools: two public and one private. To give perspective on the size of the schools, my graduating class consisted of thirty-five students. On any given Sunday morning, mostly everyone was in one of the many local churches.

While I had never known anyone who had been adopted or had adopted, the desire to adopt strongly came into my heart one day when I was young. I felt a deep, yet unknown connection to it. I was young and not even close to being able to fulfill that desire.

I grew up hearing about Jesus, but I found Him for myself at the age of twelve at my first youth camp. That's when I truly decided to follow Jesus and give Him my life, not really knowing what that meant or looked like. I thought I had connected the reason I acted the way I did with the reason I attended church. I thought I understood what it meant to be good and do good. I thought I had it figured out.

Through high school, I continued to be a good person, attended church, and even told others about Christ, but I hadn't truly surrendered my all to Him because I honestly didn't know I needed to. I had thought you took what you were good at and made the most of it. I even interpreted many verses about spiritual gifts in the Bible as showing us what talents God gave us. And with those gifts, I assumed you started a career down an obvious path...

What was I good at?

It was already evident that dreaming about my future came naturally to me, unlike most orphans and neglected children. If I had not grown up in a society where teachers and parents allowed and encouraged me to dream, my story would probably be much different.

My mom, who had always assured me I could become whatever I desired, helped me dream through high school; therefore, when I got to college, I knew immediately what I would major in—journalism! That's what I was good at. I applied to only one college, not because I was confident but because I really couldn't choose another place to go. I was so nervous when I got my "acceptance letter." This small-town girl was going to Southern Methodist University, SMU, in Dallas, Texas!

The first semester of my freshman year, I started going to the Daily Update—the student newscast required for journalism students. We had to be there by 5:45 a.m., and if anchoring, we had to wake up and arrive looking presentable. In high school, I joked with someone in the cafeteria that I would "never see a 5 on the clock in the morning." For some reason, I remember that moment because it certainly didn't last long. Not only was I seeing a 5 when waking, but I was in college! That's not something many people accomplish (except for college athletes).

From the start, I was determined to be the best I could be and to work hard to get there. Many people thought I was a junior or senior. Even my advisor forgot my year because I was doing more than required. I was going to the Daily Update because I wanted to. I stayed ahead of my major and took as many classes as possible to make room for internships during my senior year. During my junior year, I interned at CBS 11 in Dallas. Senior year, I interned at The CW 33 in Dallas and *The Today Show* with NBC in New York City. Things seemed to be working out, and this was what I was supposed to be doing with my life.

Those experiences are good examples of doing what I was supposed to do with what I was good at. For some, that may be exactly what God has prepared for you and what His plans are for your life. For others, that may only be *your* plan for your life...

In the last few months of school, as reality and graduation grew closer, I wondered whether this was it. *Was this really what I was supposed to do?* It was a now or never re-evaluation time—right before I got into the "real world."

4

In July of 2010, American visitors came to the orphanage, and one of those was Natalie. I didn't usually hang out with them, talk to them, or even introduce myself because I was so shy. Every time we had visitors, our director from the orphanage requested me to help them prepare food, so I was always in the kitchen. That was another reason I didn't talk to the Americans—because I was so busy.

I heard about someone—a visitor—named Natalie. Many kids talked about her since she was at the orphanage for five days with the medical mission instead of staying with the rest of the team who were only there for two days.

Every time I passed her, we smiled at each other. The last day before she left, she asked to take a selfie together. On the last night at our celebration, she gave the picture to me. It was so embarrassing because I thought I was so ugly in that picture! I had heard that she would return to the orphanage for three months to learn and help the orphanage, but I didn't really care because I didn't know her that well.

One day, the director told me not to go to school because we were going to the airport to pick up Natalie. On the way home, we'd stop to buy me shoes. While we were at the airport, I didn't get out of the van. When

Natalie appeared, I just smiled and said, "Hi." We ate lunch together and returned to the orphanage.

The director told me to prepare Natalie's bedding, dinner plate, and wash her dishes after she ate. She also told me to sit beside her during meals. I thought I was her servant, but I didn't care. I just wanted to help her feel at home and enjoy her time in the Philippines, especially because she was leading our devotions, conducting games and playtime, and handling movie nights. All the orphans loved to watch movies!

After a few weeks, our friendship grew. We became like best friends, even sisters. I was happy to see her every day, and we shared many conversations. Gradually, she knew my whole life story—or at least the stuff I tell people, not all the stuff on the inside. I don't know why I started to trust her, but I gave her the chance to be part of my family because she was so different. She cared more than any other person I had ever met.

She got my attention one day when she decided to be part of our school and teach, becoming one of our English and Values teachers.

It was weird because she was my friend and we ate together every day. Now, she was my teacher, too. Our changing relationship proved difficult at first, but it was a good challenge for our English skills. I often felt we had a special bond in the orphanage because we always hung out together. She let me use her cell phone and computer to play games. I knew I cared for her when I joyfully wanted to help wash her clothes, because she was new to hand washing and developed blisters!

I didn't want to have close friends because someday they would leave me and never think about me again. My parents left and never came back, and I had a hard time trusting people.

I knew it was only words without action because nothing was different after those three months when Natalie returned to the place where she belonged in America. It was painful at first, especially since she never said when she would be back.

One day, when I got home from school, some of the orphans were playing outside. When I entered the gate, a female yelled my name. I looked up and was shocked. It was Natalie! After three months, she was back. I had missed her so much and never imagined she would actually remember us and return.

She only stayed for ten days, but I was happy for the time we spent together. Everything was different. I didn't help her or fix her food because the director asked someone else to do that.

Before she left to go back to the States, I helped her pack her stuff. We were not allowed to go inside a visitor's room without permission. Though I had permission to help her, I missed curfew and was afraid to leave and be caught, so I slept in her room. I got in big trouble the next day, but I didn't regret it because that was the last opportunity to be together and talk before she left.

As the days, months, and years passed, she never forgot me. We communicated through Facebook, and one day she asked what I was going to do after I graduated with my associate's degree. I told her I wanted to help orphans like me.

5

My first day at Prestonwood, I got a call from a young woman in a severely dysfunctional relationship that she didn't know how to get out of. She confided in me. I had not experienced what she was going through, and as she shared, I prayed that God would give me the words to comfort and guide her. I told her how much God loved her and how He created her to be loved and cared for by a man and not treated as an object or toy. She wept, and I knew the Holy Spirit was working in her heart. She had never felt self-worth apart from what this man had asked of her, but she still felt empty.

I shared the love and forgiveness of Christ with her, and she decided to leave her old ways and follow Jesus. I knew God had chosen me for the position in that moment because He knew He would be in control and would guide me every day. I could not lead others through what I had never experienced without the Holy Spirit's guidance. To this day, she follows Jesus and continues to seek His love instead of a love that will not fulfill her.

Other times, God brought women to me who were broken in different ways, searching for meaning and purpose beyond their singleness. So many women feel as if they cannot live their lives until they are married. However, it's just the opposite. The present is the best time for them to live their lives. There may not be another period with that much freedom and time to serve and live. Singleness is the perfect time to serve the Lord because marriage brings other responsibilities and needed attention. Waiting for marriage may turn into regret one day if you haven't pursued your career and life aspirations.

I once heard a story about a girl who was waiting for "the one" to find her. She prayed for him day in and day out, stayed pure, and did everything she could to wait for him. Years went by... *Why couldn't he find her?* Because she was living and working in her parents' basement!

When a family comes along, focus shifts. Of course, that's a God-given shift, but He also desires everyone to have an abundant life beyond his or her wildest dreams. Just as the American Dream isn't what everyone wants or is made for. In fact, maybe the typical route for women, and even men, is not all that God has planned. He placed desires in our hearts, and He may not be telling us to wait and do something later but to do something now! I have personally experienced the joy and peace that overflow once you act on your desires. I believe the rest of life will start to make sense and the waiting will not be so tough.

I started a program while at Prestonwood entitled "Why Wait?!" to empower young singles to live now and serve now. We had several sessions, including "Why Wait to get married?" and "Why Wait until marriage?" God made your body *for* marriage and not for every guy or girl you date *until* marriage.

"Why Wait to go?" You can go anywhere now. If you're being called to go, go.

"Why Wait to share your faith?" You never know when you may be the last person someone meets who could tell them about Jesus.

"Why Wait to be a mom?" So many kids out there need a mother figure. Go and love them, serve them, mentor them, and be their big sister or brother.

"Why Wait to forgive and/or be forgiven?" Holding a grudge in your heart is only hurting yourself. Sometimes after we forgive someone, we forget to forgive ourselves.

It became clear how God was preparing me for the next venture, leading a ministry team in hopes of breaking the cycle of poverty among street kids in the Philippines through founding Streetlight, one of the first steps of Ellipsis International, in Cagayan De Oro, Philippines.

We created Streetlight to be a light among the darkness of street-life by introducing street kids to Jesus, as well as meeting their basic needs of healthcare and education. My time at Prestonwood was invaluable, resulting in lasting friendships, mentors, and experiences. Prestonwood was also the place where I met many of my best friends. That was another reason God placed me there.

I now have many life-long friends, leaders, and supporters who will always be there for me no matter where I am. It's amazing how many people forget they can communicate with you when you live in another country, but these friends never forgot.

6

I don't understand why God took my mother so early or why He did not stop. When I was ten, he took my father away, too.

In November of 2004, my family spent a night at my aunt's house. Early the next morning, my sister and I started walking home with my aunt and two cousins. Suddenly, five people showed up outside our house with guns. My sister was the only one inside the house to answer the door. I was in the back with everyone else, but we still saw them. They asked her where my father was. I was so scared I was clinging to a bamboo tree. The five people followed my sister to where we were and asked repeatedly, "Where is your father?"

Finally, my father arrived home, and they asked to talk with him for a few seconds, which turned into hours and into the night.

After their conversation, they made him kneel and tied his hands behind his back. They asked permission to take my father, but I didn't know where they were going to take him. And then he was gone.

The five people were part of the rebel army we had heard bad things about, and everyone panicked. *Where did they take my father, and why?*

Everyone in our town looked for him. That night, we didn't sleep; we cried. At midnight, my cousin came and told us my father had died from a gunshot. At that moment, I didn't know what was going to happen to me. My mom was gone, and now my dad.

The next morning, everyone was confused and shocked. We simply stared at one another.

It was two days before we saw the body of my father, and he was buried as soon as possible. Then we were told the rebels had the wrong guy. We knew they had to have been misguided. My father was a good man, and we lost him because of mistaken identity.

One month later, there was another twist in our lives. My stepmother went back to her family, and I was sent to live with my mother's brother. It was hard to live with relatives because, though we were family, we didn't fit together perfectly. Sometimes, they said things to me that made me feel like I didn't belong. I know they cared for me, but it was hard for all of us.

I was the only one sent away. The rest of my siblings stayed together with another relative. I felt abandoned.

My uncle and his family tried their best to care for me, but it became difficult for them financially. When I turned twelve, they sent me to a nearby orphanage so I could continue my education.

Once again, I felt like God took something huge away from me.

7

Throughout high school and college, I was in a relationship—for over seven years, which at that point was basically my whole life. We started dating when I was fourteen, just two years after I had given my all to Christ, but I was committed to this relationship.

At that age, it wasn't necessarily good for me to be that committed because it meant I made decisions based on the relationship and how to make it work instead of what was best for me and where God wanted to take me. The relationship became the center of my life, and it wasn't long before it took the place of Christ as top priority. The relationship pushed Jesus aside, but it happened slowly and I was so young I didn't realize what was happening.

To make a seven-year story short, I realized during my senior year that I was living my life to be with a guy and not following my dreams and God's plan for my life, and we broke up. For the first time in my life, I asked God, "What do *You* want me to do with my life?" Everything changed...

I had put God in a box to fit the mold that I thought was obvious for my life. I majored in what I was good at and graduated looking for jobs most fitting to my degree. That seems logical, right? For some, that may be exactly the path God planned. But looking back, I wish I had asked that question first.

Isaiah 55:8-9 states: "'For my thoughts are not your thoughts, neither are your ways my ways,' declares the Lord. 'As the Heavens are higher than the earth, so are my ways higher than your ways and my thoughts than your thoughts.'" When I allowed God to be creative with my life and be in control, He was!

When I asked, He reminded me of the desire to adopt. I felt Him saying, "Remember that desire to adopt a child one day? Well, that's what I want you to do with your life, and I'm going to multiply it!"

At first, I had no clue how to interpret this or even move toward doing something about it. However, I desired to go on an overseas mission trip, so I began searching.

I'll be honest with you. When my life started changing direction, I was struggling. Not only was I figuring out what I was supposed to do, I was also trying to understand where I had gone wrong in my previous relationship. *If that wasn't right, then what was? I mean, are there even any good guys out there anymore? How do you find them, and what makes them good?* I was lost because I thought I had it all figured out.

One night, while vacationing with my family in Florida in 2010, we were watching a championship football game. I was watching, but my mind struggled through the breakup and finding direction in life. The University of Florida was playing, and I listened to the commentators discuss quarterback Tim Tebow's faith. I noticed the Bible verse on his eye-black (black grease worn under an athlete's eye to reduce glare in a stadium). Sometimes players write messages on it, and his was Scripture, so I looked up the verse. I noticed another team member wearing a verse also, so I looked that one up as well. I wondered... *What makes these guys so great? What happened in their lives to cause them to be so bold for Jesus?*

I did what most people would do... I googled! I had no idea Tim Tebow was born in the Philippines, so I kept searching and reading to find out why. After I read about his family and their ministry in the Philippines, I applied for their summer mission trip, preaching the Gospel around the islands.

I always assumed I would go to Africa on a mission trip, but God had a different plan. He used something I struggled with at the time to introduce me to the Philippines. God used my relationship struggles to show me how He was going to multiply my desire to adopt.

I didn't have to apply for other mission trips because everything fell into place for the trip with the Bob Tebow Evangelistic Association (BTEA). I was accepted right away, and God quickly brought in the funding. That's how I knew, and that's why I didn't look for other options. God made it so clear! I needed Him to assure me I was on the right path. When everything fell into place, I knew God was up to something.

The organization sent an email that our team was holding a medical clinic at the BTEA orphanage (called Uncle Dick's Home) during one of the three weeks of our trip. They asked medical students to reply if they were interested in helping with the clinic. I'm not a medical student *at all*, but I was interested that they would be at the orphanage for an entire week. If you know me, you know one of my life mottos, "You never know until you try!"

So that's just what I did. I emailed back. I was honest and said if there was an opening, I would be interested in helping because I felt God called me to work with orphans and I wanted to experience as much as I could.

Lo and behold, they approved me. I stayed at the orphanage for an entire week of my three-week trip, which was supposed to be spent traveling to schools across the country and preaching the Gospel. At that point, I saw God had a reason for this trip. He had a different agenda—a bigger plan for that week than I could imagine. I prayed that week, intently asking the Lord to reveal the truth about the lives of orphans. I asked Him to help me not just *see* their reality but *feel* it in a deep, true way, not in a warm, fuzzy way.

8

The first day at the orphanage, the new rules confused me. I was suddenly staying with strangers, sleeping next to people I didn't know, and calling a woman I barely knew, "Mom." My first thought was, *That's why I am here... to gain an uncle to help me through my education.* The orphanage's name was Uncle Dick's Home, so I assumed I had an uncle named Uncle Dick.

The first night at dinner, I was shocked. Almost sixty people ate together, including the staff. That many people intimidated me.

I arrived in the summer, and every day we cleaned the grounds of the orphanage, including sweeping dirt and leaves from pathways to the buildings, to town, and to the school. Compared to home, a lot more work was necessary. I struggled, missing home as I adapted, but it wasn't too long before I got used to things.

Every now and then, I would make a mistake at school or be disrespectful toward our houseparents. But I was determined that no matter what it took, I would work hard so I could finish my studies.

Once class started in June, I couldn't believe I was attending school for the first time with all the necessary supplies. I had a new school bag, the required notebooks, proper shoes, and pencils. I had never experienced that before. I felt like a rich kid going to school. I no longer had to worry about finding money to pay for projects, food, and clothing. Even though I couldn't pick what I ate, I was thankful I was never hungry.

One day, some orphans decided to run away, and I helped. I wondered whether I should go with them, but I thought my uncle would be mad at me. Since I didn't have enough money to take a bus and had a place to stay, I decided not to join them.

Every year, the orphanage held Family Day, when relatives visited. We had activities planned throughout the day for which we had practiced for many months. None of my relatives showed. Each time, I hoped someone would remember me and miraculously arrive.

I shifted my focus to the orphanage and became one of the orphans with the most responsibility. Our director trusted me with things, like accompanying her to buy groceries and running errands. That brought me joy because I felt important and needed. Every time we had visitors, Nanay (Filipino for "mother") asked me to help. I felt lucky that out of fifty other orphans, she chose me.

9

We landed in the smallest airport I had ever been to in General Santos City on the island of Mindanao, which is the second largest island and one of the southern-most islands in the Philippines. Seven major languages are spoken on that island alone, with many more dialects deep into the mountains. The Philippines was thirteen hours ahead of home, so most everyone was asleep as we drove the couple of hours to the orphanage, but I was wide awake.

The landscape was beautiful, unlike anything I had ever seen. We passed through a small city and journeyed up the mountain. It was as if we were driving through the jungle but on a mountain, which was foreign to me. The only mountains I had seen were snowy or covered with evergreens. Vibrant flowers and plants strategically lined the sides of the road as if to welcome us. Farther inland, fields of green squares were all around us. I learned they were fields of rice— very fitting for the Philippines, and Asia for that matter!

It was evident God was going to speak to me at the orphanage and reveal something big. I prayed the whole way that He would allow me to experience Himself and the lives of the children in a way other than what I had experienced before. The road curved, and around the corner, a little village popped up. We slowed down, and my heart sped up. *Here we go!*

When I stepped from the van, children ran toward us. As I stood there, I felt it—something different, new. It sounds odd, but I had a profound feeling I would connect with them and understand them, for a reason I did not yet know. God had answered my prayer that very moment, and I saw the orphanage in a different light than most.

I wondered... *What does it feel like when people who appear to have perfect lives and families visit an orphanage?* I tried to see beyond the happiness I felt on this trip. I thought of the kids and their lives. How did they deal with what they had been through and what they saw in us?

That week, God opened my eyes, and I felt Him showing me there was something more to this trip. Immediately, I prayed for a chance to talk with Mr. Tebow about my newfound desire to help and love orphans.

One morning, our team arrived at the site for the medical clinic. I commented to a friend that if I went missing, I would be climbing a nearby breathtaking mountain.

He replied with laughter in his voice, "Good luck in those shoes!"

I looked down to find I was wearing my shower shoes, which were not allowed at the medical clinic! I couldn't believe I had forgotten to change shoes. That's not like me!

I asked Eddie, one of the translators, if he could take me back to the orphanage to change. He happened to be heading that way to pick up Mr. Tebow. At that moment, I knew this was an answer to prayer.

At the orphanage, I sprinted to get my shoes. I didn't want him to think I was irresponsible. Once we were back in the car, Mr. Tebow joked, "Forget something?"

I knew it was now or never. I shared with Mr. Tebow my desire to help orphans but that I didn't know how to pray about it.

Immediately, as if he were waiting for me to ask, he replied, "Well, I think you're all right, so why don't you come back here?"

Did I hear that correctly? He didn't even answer my question about how to pray about this. Clearly, this was an answer to my prayers and actually God speaking through Him. I screamed within.

He invited me to spend a longer time at the orphanage, to explore and learn more about what God called me to do. Instead of analyzing what was in my heart, we decided I should jump in and discover firsthand the Master's plan. It was evident this was a divine conversation.

After that conversation, my mind raced. I was so excited, and I experienced a peace that this was the path God had for me, at least for now. It was hard to keep it to myself, but I wanted time to pray through it and tell my family face-to-face.

The next time I talked on the telephone with my family and they asked how everything was going, I had to leave out a few details...

I simply said, "It is going great." *They had no idea exactly how great!* I wasn't quite sure how they'd react to the news. Of course, they would probably think I was crazy going back to the Philippines and spending so much time there right after college rather than job-hunting, especially after my internship in NYC. I prayed they'd understand, the same way God had given me peace and understanding.

10

Living in the orphanage was fun and exciting, but there were also rules to follow that were not so fun. I knew it was best for us, but we always dreamed of families that would give us more freedom and less rules. Nevertheless, it was very memorable.

I was there for six years. I learned how to be a good person, how to take care of myself, how to serve God, and how to be wise. Still, on the inside, there was pain. I was far from my family and relatives, and no one ever visited me. Sometimes, it was hard to fight and to want to live. Many times, I planned to run away or ask for termination in order to leave. I don't know where I would have gone. I always stayed in hopes of a brighter future. Because of the orphanage, I finished college. The orphanage helped me grow as a person and prepared me for my future.

I changed a lot while living at the orphanage. I didn't have any family there like the other kids with siblings. It was so different from where I grew up that they even spoke a different language! When my uncle took me there, I went without hesitation because I knew I needed a new life and a new "family."

Although I didn't see my siblings while in the orphanage, God put people in my life who took good care of me. He gave me many brothers and sisters who were orphans like me. I have been through countless difficult situations, but I was able to face them with God, whom I accepted as my Savior while at the orphanage. Even though I sometimes ignored Him, God showed me His love every day. I needed His help to see the end or the bright side of my suffering, but I couldn't always see it.

After college, He provided a person to take care of me, who gave me everything I would need. I felt the love of the people He chose to care for me.

Natalie helped me realize my passion to care for children with similar stories and experiences to mine. When I turned nineteen, I worked toward that goal. Since then, I have been walking with God faithfully and will always be thankful for the people He gave me to help me find my purpose in life in spite of what I went through to get here.

11

When I returned home from the Philippines, I vividly remember sitting down with my parents in the living room to prepare them for what I would do next.

I looked at them with a big smile on my face and said, "I'm going back... for three months... in six weeks!"

My dad's jaw nearly hit the floor. I had never seen them so shocked. They knew I would want to go back, but they had no idea it would be so soon and for so long.

Once again, people were confused and shocked at the turn my life was taking. It was totally opposite from *The Today Show*, but I knew it was right! I faced a lot of reservation and even opposition, but God gave me the strength to stand strong and peace as I prepared. I was following God, and if He wanted me to apply for jobs in journalism after the three months, then I would. I had already learned the hard way what happens when you lose focus.

People continued to believe I was "losing it" and that I was throwing everything away, including my college degree, because of a breakup. They thought I was walking away from an amazing opportunity to capitalize on my internship in NYC. However, I had to explore this newfound desire while I had the chance. Looking back, there is no greater time to do something before entering "the real world." It was my last chance to explore this desire before society said, "Settle down."

Little did I know I was embarking on a journey that would shape me and teach me in more ways than school or a job. My experiences gave me what a classroom or degree could not.

In the Philippines, I met mothers, fathers, business owners, farmers, students, educators, those with little and those with abundance, and I found we're all the same yet vastly different. But the differences are much deeper than the obvious. The biggest difference is that many of the people I met never had a choice about the course of their life, and therefore, never had a chance to dream.

They were getting an education; some had families; others had jobs; yet few were living their dream— because they had never dreamed! *Imagine a life without dreams.*

For the most part, I don't dream at night. Many doctors would say it's not that I don't dream but that I don't remember my dreams. Nevertheless, I always felt left out on the playground when my friends shared their dreams from the previous night. That was an unfortunate feeling growing up. Imagine living a life where no one asked you what your real dreams or life goals were or, worse yet, one where you didn't know you *could* dream...

Yes, God is sovereign and knows where we will be born, and we cannot change the situation into which we are born. God also enables those of us who have dreamed to dream for those who don't—to go to them and give them a chance to dream and a choice for their future. It's not that they were never meant to dream; they've just never met the Dream Maker who made them for a reason.

12

At the orphanage, we treated each other as sisters and brothers. At first, I didn't want to call anyone else my brother or sister, but when I did, it helped me feel as if I had a family. They were all I had, and we found comfort in each other because we were all the same. We were orphans.

When we went to the mall, we saw many children our age with moms and dads. They were buying them whatever they wanted. If we were together, it was much easier to accept we didn't have that and be thankful for what the orphanage gave us.

Our school also had a Family Day program. Our parents, of course, didn't come to that either. We would look at each other and say, "It's okay." We tried to laugh when we noticed we were different from everyone else at school. They all knew we were orphans. They knew about our rules, too, and would often talk about how we had so many things to do in order to stay out of trouble. The orphanage was so many things in one: a home, a school, a church. We never did anything at night unless it was for church.

One day, one of my sisters at the orphanage read a book about romance. Our rules said we couldn't read outside books, so we hid the book under our bed until the houseparents turned out the lights. Then all the older girls, including me, read it. One night, the houseparents were smarter than we were and came in our room after the lights were out and caught us. Once our houseparents found out, we were in big trouble.

The next morning, the houseparents said we would not be going to school. Our punishment was to dig a big hole for our garbage. Even though we were being punished, we found a way to have fun together and laugh about it. Looking back, I think I dug a hole five times from breaking the rules. However, just because we laughed about it didn't mean it was easy. We only had a shovel, and the ground was hard. We learned the book wasn't worth it.

13

When I arrived back in the Philippines in September of 2010, I was greeted at the airport by familiar faces, all of whom I recognized as staff. When I got in the van with my things, I looked in the back and saw a giggling young girl, who had been one of the staff members who helped prepare and serve our meals the previous summer. I smiled at her and said hello. We had not really spoken before. She was painfully shy.

We drove away from the airport but stopped halfway to eat lunch, and "Nanay," which is Filipino for mother (pronounced nigh-NIY with a long "i" sound), had to buy some things at the store. The young girl, Brindy, went inside with Nanay, and they returned about an hour later with shoes for Brindy and a few of the kids. That's when I realized Brindy wasn't staff!

We were back on the road, and I was eager to see the kids again. Little did I know the girl sitting behind me would change my life.

The van pulled in the familiar driveway, and slowly but surely, little people appeared at the windows, stairs, and by the trees to say hello to "Ate" Natalie!

When someone visits the Philippines, he/she learns quickly that everyone is either an "Ate" (pronounced Ah-teh) or a "Kuya" (pronounced KOU-yah), which translates as older sister or older brother. It is not literal, but a form of endearment and seniority, even when the age difference is merely a year or two.

The embraces that ensued are forever ingrained in my mind. From the moment I stepped out of the van, God changed the course of what I thought my life was supposed to be.

I was actually here! I came back to them. I wondered what the kids felt after meeting so many foreigners every summer, not knowing if they would ever see them again. I was lucky to be able to stay long enough to get to know the kids and the staff.

Nanay led me to my room, and Kay and Angie, two of the girls at the orphanage, helped me unpack. All of a sudden, the two little girls yelled something in Illonggo (the local language), and the building shook. They ran out of the room, and I was in shock, trying to figure out what was happening. Then it hit me (not literally, thankfully). An earthquake! That was the first one I had experienced. On top of that, I didn't know the language at that point, so I was left to chance, I guess you could say.

A minute later, the little girls popped their faces into my window and said "earthquake" in broken English. *Yeah, thanks a lot now that it's over!* I smiled. That was indeed a one-of-a-kind welcoming.

After the earthquake, not wanting to waste time, I talked with Nanay about my three months. She asked me point-blank, "Why did you come here, and what do you want to do?"

I simply said, "I came to help." Deep down, I had no purpose other than to help, to love, to serve, and to learn.

We discussed different ways I could help, and one of those ways was teaching English at the local high school. This was another thing I never dreamed I would do, but before I arrived in the Philippines, I vowed I would say yes to every opportunity.

That first week, I met the principal and teachers to discuss the teaching opportunity, and the current English teacher, Ma'am Tupas, handed me her books...

Wait, what?

She said, "You start Monday."

Well, I guess I'm a teacher now!

I had the chance to meet many kids through that class, whom I still keep in touch with to this day. We had fun, they learned, and we made lifelong relationships.

One of the main reasons I wanted to get involved in the school was to share the Gospel. I knew I'd be able to share with the orphans, but I wanted to share with the community as well. This connection allowed me to meet with other classes, and before long, my "job" expanded. I taught Moral Values to the entire high school. Twice a week, I rotated through the classes before school started and taught a Bible lesson based around a moral value. That was the way I shared the Gospel.

Ask and you shall receive.

14

While I was at the orphanage, I didn't care about anything. It was okay for me to eat anything, say anything, and think anything. I never worried about my future or how I would sustain myself after I was discharged. I lived one day at a time.

Before the orphanage, I had nothing. We were so poor that I had one pair of shoes, a pair of pants, and two shirts. I went to school and then washed and wore everything, repeatedly. I had no breakfast, no lunch, and no allowance to go to school. School required us to have two notebooks and one pencil. Because we didn't have schoolbags, we used cellophane or plastic bags from the local market after buying vegetables.

Even still, I wished my parents had never been taken away. Because it was hard to deal with, I often became angry and asked God why He let that happen to me. I couldn't see how it would ever help me. I thought about it every day and woke up every morning hoping it was all a dream.

When I met Natalie, she helped me understand how God could use my life for good. It took many years, and I am still learning more every day. Not only was Natalie my guardian, but my family, too. She took care of me. The most precious gift God gave me was to be part of her family and enjoy life.

Even though I once felt alone in this world, I now feel like a princess. I have plenty of shoes, bags, and dresses. I now feel important.

15

In 2011, I tried to organize a mission trip to the Philippines with some of my friends from Young Singles at Prestonwood. Every group I tried to coordinate kept falling apart until, finally, I felt God telling me to take my family to the Philippines. They needed to see where I was, with whom I lived, and why I'd been called there long-term.

At Christmastime, I gathered my family so I could discuss something with them. As they sat around in the living room, they knew something was up!

We had just finished our tradition of reading the Christmas story of Jesus' birth. I sat in my usual spot on the couch arm (which typically means I don't want to sit down all the way because I have a story to tell).

"God has told me that instead of taking a group of friends to the Philippines, I need to take y'all! So, we're going to the Philippines sometime this year!" I shared with a confident grin on my face and a big "ta-da" arm gesture of sheer excitement.

They were flattered and thought it was the sweetest idea but didn't see how that would be possible with schedules and finances. The Philippines was a long way to go for five people on the same budget, but I knew it would happen because God told me it would. I kept praying and believing it.

Months went by, and though we didn't forget, the trip moved farther and farther out of reach. There was only one window of time when everyone could be free to go, and six weeks before the target date of departure, my dad called me. His first words were, "We're going to the Philippines!" I knew what that meant and how huge an answer to prayer it was. He'd been able, finally, to sell a business he had been trying to sell for years, and our trip depended upon that sale. God's faithfulness was the only explanation.

This was the trip of a lifetime! I showed my family where I lived in 2010 and where I learned God's destiny for me. They saw first-hand where I'd found my purpose. They met everyone, including Brindy.

On this short trip, God did more than show my family where my heart was and reunite me with my friends. He opened the door to my future, and my family received a front-row seat to watch the journey begin.

During the trip, I had several meetings lined up with other organizations in the Philippines. I wanted to network and build relationships for the far-away future. I loved my job at Prestonwood and wasn't ready to move to the Philippines, but I wanted to at least meet other organizations that might need long-term help.

Unfortunately, every single meeting fell through. The next morning, I got up early, sat with God, and prayed for clarity. I prayed for an answer and for things to work out. I was discouraged and even questioned God. "Why did you bring me here with my family to let my plans fall apart?"

The answer: God wanted to make it easy on me... He narrowed down my options.

In Manila, we stayed with Kids International Ministries (K.I.M.), an organization I was connected with by an International Mission Board family on their furlough in 2012 at Prestonwood. On my last day in

Manila, I finally got a chance to speak with Jeff, the founder of K.I.M. This was the only meeting that didn't fall through, because it couldn't—we were staying at the same place as Jeff was.

Jeff took us on a tour of the ministry site. I seized this opportunity to talk with him about my passion for orphans and neglected kids, similar to the time I talked with Mr. Tebow. I simply shared my passion and explained that I didn't know what to do about it.

He said, "Do you want to help orphans from the Philippines or from the States?"

I replied, "Here in the Philippines, and all I know is that God has called me to the island of Mindanao."

He stopped and looked at me. "I've actually been looking and praying for someone to start a ministry for street kids in Cagayan De Oro on the island of Mindanao."

It was one of those moments like, "What did you say?" I thought for sure it was too good to be true...

He suggested we change our flights and visit Cagayan De Oro, which many people refer to as CDO. My dad and I visited the city, and that was all it took. I experienced that feeling when you know something is right. I felt the same when I went to SMU for the first time. I just knew!

It was so perfect. My family not only saw the Philippines and understood the need but also witnessed God opening that door for me. None of us could deny God had orchestrated this.

16

Through teaching moral values at Lamsugod National High School in the Philippines, I met Marry Ann.

Marry Ann was one of my students and spoke better English than anyone I had met at the school. I was drawn to her from the beginning. She heard I had a degree in journalism and asked me to help her start a school newspaper.

Marry Ann and I met together several times over the next three months. We laughed, conducted mock interviews, and built a relationship, creating a legacy that she would leave at the school. By the time I left the Philippines, we had successfully made the school's first publication.

The next time I visited the orphanage a year and a half later, I visited Marry Ann. I walked through the neighborhood with one of the other kids to reach Marry Ann's house on the edge of the small town. We found a bamboo fence surrounding a traditional Filipino home constructed from coconut lumber and bamboo. Marry Ann's mother invited us in and called her to join us. I noticed immediately that something had happened to Marry Ann. She was smaller. Freshly healed scars discolored her beautiful light brown face. The previous summer, she had been helping her family on the farm when she was in a motorcycle accident. Still, she was beautiful and brilliant, but there was a sense of sadness about her and more to the story.

While we sat and talked, pride radiated from Marry Ann's mom, and I noticed how that pride was displayed on the coconut-lumber walls. Dozens of medals lined the walls among framed portraits of her graduations from elementary and high school, including awards and certificates.

One of them in particular caught my eye, and I interrupted the conversation. "Marry Ann, you were Valedictorian?" I asked excitedly, but I wasn't shocked. I knew she was sharp, but what an amazing accomplishment.

She glanced at the certificate and humbly laughed when she looked in my direction.

"What are you going to study in college?" I asked enthusiastically.

Her gaze turned to the floor as she sighed, revealing a weakness I hadn't noticed before. She mustered strength and composure to say confidently, "I'm not going to college..."

My heart sank. I couldn't believe what I had heard. *This can't be true.*

She explained how the accident caused her family to sell one of their farm animals to pay for the damages and hospital bills. That cow was a year of her college tuition. Until the family could save enough money to pay for school, she wouldn't be able to go.

I couldn't imagine her working in her family's rice and cornfields when she had the potential to be whatever she wanted. I had to do something.

All I knew to do was ask for help. I wrote a blog post about Marry Ann, praying someone would make the sacrifice to bless her with a brighter future. I believed someone would care.

I had asked what she would study if she were able to go to college, and her answer motivated me more: she wanted to be a lawyer or an accountant. I envisioned the influence her sweet spirit and her kind heart would have in those occupations. Someway, somehow, God would provide.

And He did. Several people reached out after I posted the blog. All she needed was an opportunity and someone with the power to help.

Today, Marry Ann is on her way to becoming an accountant—all because someone believed in her. She's one of many who deserve the opportunity to reach her full potential.

17

Growing up as an orphan... I will never truly know what that feels like. I can't imagine. I can't undo a child losing his parents. I can't adopt every child, yet I have a burden on my heart to do something...

I can spread a movement of love and hope to *The Forgotten Ones*, both orphaned and neglected. Anyone can make a difference by caring for one child at a time, whether physically, emotionally, or spiritually. Each child has a different story; however, it's how they move forward in the journey that matters most. Many get bogged down in the trauma they have experienced. They need to be freed from that in order to be able to live their lives.

For some children, their parents were lost in a tragic accident. Others were abandoned because they weren't wanted. That's what happened to Billy. He was a result of infidelity. We met on my first trip to the Philippines.

If only his parents could see him now: the adorable, smart young man he is becoming. By the time I went back for my three-month stay, his caretakers had potty-trained him and taught him how to cry and laugh on cue. All before he was walking!

I pray that as he grows, he will have people to encourage him through his story rather than around it. The sooner he understands that the way he entered this world does not define his life, the better. Otherwise, he'll be haunted for the rest of his life. He will struggle with ideas such as *Why am I here? Do I matter? Why didn't God just let me die when I was a baby? No one wants me. I'm worthless.*

These ideas—these lies—will torment him if no one helps him see that is not who he is. He is a child of God who has a purpose far beyond his circumstances. It's easier said than done, but step number one is recognizing and accepting reality in order to attempt to understand and even overcome or utilize the past.

Karl was another little boy I met on my first trip. I helped him every day with his math homework, and he became more interested in the subject. Karl was full of energy, by far the fastest of all the boys, with a genuine heart. One of the first things I noticed was his smile. The second was his scars.

People hesitated to ask about his scars because they didn't want to hurt his feelings by bringing up bad memories. However, I believe his story pointed out that his life had purpose. So I asked.

When Karl was an infant, he and his parents were riding in a jeepney—the most commonly used form of transportation in the Philippines. A jeepney is similar to a bus and will stop anywhere you want to get off, no matter how fast the vehicle is going when you ask to stop. Imagine an open-air, cram-packed mini-bus that looks like an elongated jeep. To get in, you climb in the back through an opening and sit sideways on one of two long benches, one on each side. If the jeep is full, you'll see people riding on the roof.

Karl and his parents were on a normal commute in the jeepney, when the driver took a sharp curve and lost control. The jeepney rolled down a mountain. The story, from my understanding, was that Karl's parents threw him out of the jeepney when they realized what was happening, in order to save his life. Karl's parents died in the crash.

Karl is still here today, and in my opinion, those scars are constant reminders of what is to come and what God is going to do through Karl. This young boy has a gift of powerful prayer; he turns a blessing of food before dinner into a beautiful and genuine prayer when oftentimes the kids want to hurry and eat. Many of the kids joke that he will become a pastor one day. Maybe so! Karl can see his scars as a reminder of the day he lost his parents, or he can see them as a reminder of how God spared his life and use that as motivation to live each day searching for purpose.

No one can take away what orphans and neglected children around the world have been through, but we can change the way they view themselves, their lives, their purpose, and how they can use it for their good and to help others. Outlook is everything, and it changes tremendously who they may become.

18

There was one orphan in particular at Uncle Dick's Home who would forever change my life. You may remember the young girl who was in the van when I arrived for my three-month stay—Brindy. I had mistaken her for a staff member when we first met because they gave her so many responsibilities. Brindy delivered all my meals, and her assigned seat was next to mine. For the first week, she barely looked up from her plate. I couldn't get her to talk, but that didn't stop me. I talked to her anyway though she just giggled and kept eating.

Once she warmed up to me, she loved the fact that I couldn't understand the language. She and her friends would have long conversations and, every now and then, look over at me and giggle. I'd ask what they were talking about, and she would always respond with, "Gwapa ka," which means, "You're pretty." I assumed they were talking about how differently I looked, but it was a copout so they wouldn't have to explain what they were actually talking about. It took me years to figure that out. Now that I speak the language, that trick doesn't work anymore.

Over time, Brindy talked to me more often. She was also one of my students, so I'd pick on her in class sometimes just because she was so painfully shy. Something about her drew me in, and it wasn't long before we were inseparable. We were buddies. If I needed to go somewhere, I took her with me, and we became like sisters.

I remember one night toward the end of my stay when we were walking home from an event. The footpath we followed was only a couple of feet wide, created by numerous locals going to and from their daily jobs. It was dark, so she held my arm while we dodged cow droppings and bumps along the way. Because there was no light, we saw the stars clearly, which was one of my favorite things to do at the edge of the orphanage property. The sky was remarkably clear and beautiful.

I was telling Brindy about the tradition of making a wish when you see a shooting star. Unbelievably at that moment, a star flew across the sky, and we both saw it and gasped. We each made a wish. I don't know what her wish was, but mine has already come true.

19

Once I finished my associate's degree, more blessings came. I never imagined that after the orphanage I'd be able to live with someone else, which would make me feel free. I had no hesitation at all. This was the right path for me. I was eighteen years old and thought I was a grownup and could survive on my own.

A few days after I moved, I questioned why my parents died so early and why I was the only one separated from my siblings and relatives. Why didn't they come to see me or communicate with me?

Those thoughts ate me alive. I was so angry with God that I almost hated Him. No one could explain my feelings. I was eighteen, but my emotions were much younger.

For all those years, I had covered up my feelings. That's why, when I was out of the orphanage, I struggled to deal with my past. It was almost worse than when my parents died.

Because of my emotional barriers, Natalie struggled to deal with me. She unlocked these emotions when she encouraged me to visit my family. Every time she talked about my past, I changed the subject or ignored her. Those questions made me think about my previous life, and I didn't want to remember. I just wanted to move on.

It turned out I couldn't move on. I felt crazy inside. I couldn't control my emotions or thoughts, and they were destroying me. I felt alone even though Natalie sat next to me. I felt like no one cared, especially my siblings. However, I didn't know their story or if they were even still alive. Most likely, they didn't have the money for a bus ride to where I had lived for six years. Still, it was hard not to think that I didn't matter to them.

I tried to keep everything to myself. I would rather not trust anyone or become close with anyone because I was scared of losing people again. I wanted a normal life with a mother, father, and siblings.

20

The last week of my three-month stay proved very eventful when I was asked to do something I had never done before: sing and preach at a funeral. And not one, but two.

Because I'm an American, the locals found it special for me to be a part of their events. From the beginning, I had decided I would say yes to every opportunity. However, I never pictured that would involve funerals.

Someone had heard me sing at an event the previous week so the family assumed I'd love to sing at their father's funeral. I didn't know them, but if it was special to them, then I would do it.

Surprisingly, I wasn't too nervous waiting for the part of the ceremony when I would sing. Someone obviously had discovered the song I'd planned to sing because when I stood, the individual on the piano started to play "Amazing Grace." To most, this would have been a nice surprise, but it was quite the hurdle. I'm not quite sure I made it over this one...

You see, I like to sing "Amazing Grace" in a lower key. When I got to the bridge of Chris Tomlin's version, let's just say I had a "Mariah Carey moment," exactly what I wish I'd sounded like (instead of a squeaky mouse), as cell phones and video cameras could have captured my entry video into the Philippines' funniest home videos.

The song abruptly ended after the chorus as I bowed my head in gratitude and darted to my seat, beet-red, to find Brindy holding her breath to control her laughter. She was almost as red as I was. Most people had no idea anything went wrong except the orphans and staff who had heard me before and knew something was off. Tatay, which means "father" in Filipino, leaned around Brindy and said with a sly but polite grin, "A little high?" With that, Brindy and I folded over our knees to hide our uncontrollable laughter. Needless to say, since then I have declined all invitations to sing in public. Don't even ask!

To top it off, on my very last day, we boarded a jeepney that was actually the size of about two normal jeepneys to attend a funeral where I was asked to preach. Thankfully, this one didn't involve singing. The super-sized jeepney was packed with people, food, and clothes. We were going to the other side of the valley, but I didn't expect to get there the way we did. I'm surprised we made it at all!

We drove down a concrete road that turned to dirt, but that was expected. We approached the river. No bridge in sight. The road, however, continued on the other side. One would assume, since the bridge was out, that we needed to detour, but the driver wasn't slowing down, and he forded the river. It happened too fast for me to react with anything but shock. I looked around to see if anyone else was worried, but no one flinched.

Reaching the other side should have felt relieving, but the experience escalated while driving up the mountain, all but turning over sideways. I'm not sure how we survived that journey.

If you've never been to the Philippines, let me tell you, you must take your own toilet paper wherever you go, and sometimes no bathroom exists. Great experience for my last day. After the long trek across the river, I tried to hold it... But when you gotta go— *you gotta go*! I looked around at the bamboo huts and hoped someone would have a CR ("comfort room," as they call it).

My local friends helped me communicate with the people in this community, the T'Boli. They pointed to the woods and laughed, but I wasn't afraid to go there. Still true—when you gotta go! Then a grinning woman motioned us to follow her, almost as if she felt privileged to open her home for the American to pee.

We walked into her bamboo hut, which consisted of two rooms, and she pointed to the corner, saying in broken English, "Here. Just Here." Before I could comprehend or react, she was gone. I stood alone in her house, pondering what to do, since this was her *home* and what she had pointed to was not a toilet but a corner of the room. There was a bed in each room, with mats for sleeping and kids' clothes neatly folded in a bucket on the bed nearest me. "*Is this someone's bedroom?*" I whispered in horror. My bladder reminded me time was running out.

One other important aspect to note is that the walls of these homes didn't reach the floor, leaving a few inches for the rain to pass through. Therefore, while my bladder was about to burst, I had to decide what was worse—to be miserable for several more hours, distracted while preaching, and try to hold it while going down the mountain, or try to forget that people stood on the other side of the wall who would see a man-made river flowing past their feet...

I did the unthinkable and created a river in their home. I'm not sure this experience can ever be trumped! That family and I have a bond that cannot be broken. Think what you want to think.

After that, it was time for the funeral. On a more serious note, I was honored to have the opportunity to share the peace that we have in death if we know Jesus. As I shared, I paused often for the pastor to translate from English to Ilonggo and then another translator to translate into T'Boli. It was an incredible experience for my message to be translated into three languages. Truly, I will never forget that community for that experience; however, I do hope there is at least one small detail they will forget!

21

I rode a huge airplane for the first time and had my own TV. I've been to Japan; at least, I visited the airport. The best part was when I stepped off the plane in America. I was so overwhelmed I couldn't believe what I was seeing. I thought I was dreaming! Natalie's family welcomed us at the airport with balloons and gifts. Mary Frances, Natalie's sister, brought me a scarf made to look like the American flag, which she wrapped around me. They also brought us jackets because it was my first winter. I felt so famous, that I was a part of their family!

On our trip, we went to different churches to talk about our ministry and my story. Those experiences helped me gain confidence in myself. I learned a lot and met many new people.

One week, they took me to "the happiest place on earth"—Disney World. I couldn't believe what I saw. It was the most interesting place, and I felt so special. For the first time, I encountered real happiness because Natalie's family was there with me. That was the first time in a long time I experienced family who embraced me as a sister and a daughter.

The memories we made on that trip will be cherished in my heart forever. We rode many rides, saw different shows, and ate lots of good food. Natalie's family totally accepted me for who I was and helped me understand myself. We even wore t-shirts that Natalie made for my birthday, with my famous saying on them: "It's part of growing up." I used that phrase when things needed to be done that we didn't want to do, which made Natalie and her mom laugh.

They didn't make me feel different from them. This was a new feeling that helped me learn I was loved and that God still had a plan for me. He gave me a new family.

22

Every child should be entitled to dream, to wish, and to want. Even if nothing comes from it, it teaches them to have hope beyond the here and now...

In Hebrews 11:1, God encourages us to have hope: "Faith is the confidence that what we hope for will actually happen; it gives us assurance about things we cannot see." Faith and hope go hand in hand. If we want to teach kids to have faith, we must also teach them to have hope.

In the orphanage, when I asked the kids to turn in their assignments about what they wanted to be when they grew up, the only one who did not give me her assignment was Brindy. She said she would give it to me before I left for the U.S., saying she didn't want me to read it until after I'd gone. She gave it to me the last day, and of course, that night I read it.

Brindy helped me pack, and after we finished, I told her I had read her letter. She was shy at first, but I told her I had been praying for her because I felt God was going to use her and her story in an amazing way. God was going to use us together somehow, but I didn't want to say anything before knowing her heart and her personal dreams. I didn't want to influence her if God wasn't calling her to work alongside me.

Her dream letter began with finishing school, getting a good job, and seeing her siblings again. What answered my prayer was the very last sentence.

She had written: "And one day, I want to help orphans just like me."

I said, "I don't know when or where, but I know one day we will be able to help orphans and neglected kids together."

I'll never forget that conversation because I made her a promise, and I didn't want to promise more than I knew to be true. That's all I knew at the time, but I was hopeful. I tried to teach her how to be hopeful and how to trust again, when someone cares for you and wants to help you.

Brindy and I kept in touch while I was in America working at Prestonwood. The moment I realized God was calling me back, I sent her a message asking her once again what she wanted to do when she was finished with her associate's degree. Her reply was the same, "I want to help orphans just like me." What an amazing testimony of her heart. Though she had an education and could get a job doing anything, she still wanted to help others.

The three months I stayed at her orphanage changed my life, shaped me for what God had planned, and allowed me to build relationships that would last a lifetime. This particular relationship turned into family as God grew us closer together over time. Not only was Brindy like a sister to me, she was an encourager, a catalyst, and an inspiration.

23

When I opened my Facebook one day, I received a message that Natalie would be visiting the orphanage with her family in 2012. They visited our school to see me, and I felt so special. I met her brother, sister, mother, and father. After that visit, though, she left me again.

When she visited, she had good news that she would be moving to the Philippines one day, and I was overloaded with happiness. She even invited me to live with her. At that time, I realized that despite everything I had been through, she still loved me for who I was.

God changed my life after this message from Natalie. I was excited to graduate with an associate's degree because I wanted to live with her. I didn't know why she wanted me to live with her, but probably it was because she loved me and never stopped believing in me even though I wasn't perfect. She never received anything from me in return, but God continued to bless me with her.

On my graduation day, she walked with me down the aisle. At first, it was embarrassing because everyone stared at us, but I felt special because she was there to celebrate my success. Everyone else had their moms and dads walk with them. For me, Natalie *was* my family.

Every kid, every orphan, deserves the happiness family brings and the opportunity to follow their dreams. One day, I hope kids similar to me will encounter people who can help them like Natalie helped me. She changed my life. She helped me become strong and independent. She stood in the hole in my life as my mother and sister because she fulfilled what my life was missing at that time. She was an angel sent by God. I was a normal kid with a big dream that I'd never have discovered without the hope Natalie gave me.

24

After the trip to the Philippines with my family, I went back to work at Prestonwood Baptist Church. I prayed daily about what God revealed to me in the Philippines, but I was scared. Thoughts flooded my mind: *Is this really it? Why now? I've only had my job for a little over a year, and I've invested so much in these women. I don't want to abandon them.*

Then Satan filled my head with lies and twisted logic: "You'll be forgotten. You'll lose all your friends... you'll be alone. You're leaving your family. You're going to miss everything. No one will keep in touch with you. And... you'll NEVER get married!"

Many sleepless and painful nights followed when I cried out to God to help me understand. I felt myself dying, dying to everything I thought was my own and everything I had been holding onto. It was excruciating. My grieving was like grieving the death of a loved one because I grieved my own life. Like Jesus says in Luke 9:23: "If anyone would come after me, let him deny himself and take up his cross daily and follow me." The cost of following Jesus is *daily* denial of oneself. I experienced this to my core. I knew we were to give up a lot to follow Jesus, but I never imagined I would truly feel myself dying.

In 2 Corinthians 4:16, it makes more sense why this is necessary: "So we do not lose heart. Though our outer self is wasting away, our inner self is being renewed day by day." Each day, God chiseled away the life I had become comfortable with so I would be ready for the life He had for me.

It's a reality check to look back and see that God had to rid me of myself so dramatically twice in my life. This proves how easy it is to fall back into following one's own path instead of God's. I thought that after losing myself by placing a guy before the Lord in a seven-year relationship that I would never follow my own ways again. And though I do not believe I *wasn't* following Jesus, I had become comfortable in serving Him right where I was in Plano, Texas, not too far away from my family. I may have missed this opportunity to help kids in the Philippines had I not held my life in a loose grip. This time, I was more open to allowing the Lord to change my path and mold my direction even though I was nervous.

That summer was a battle. Amidst the battle, I flew to Kansas for an interview with the K.I.M. board members. I trusted their judgment on whether or not they thought I was ready and if I was the one to start this ministry for street kids in CDO. They were worried because I was a young, single female.

After much prayer and two months of waiting, I was ready. I decided that this was it, and I would follow if the board opened the doors for me.

A couple of months after the interview, my family visited me in Texas for the Fourth of July weekend. On July 5, 2012, the day they were leaving, I woke up feeling compelled to pray that I would hear something, *anything*, from the board. Unbelievably, that afternoon, I received a message that they wanted to call me. I scheduled the call for after my family got on the road for Mississippi.

I was nervous. The phone rang. I answered, and immediately Keith, one of the board members, said, "We want to welcome you to the K.I.M. family!"

I was speechless. I was overwhelmed with joy and couldn't believe it. I immediately called my family. There was excitement, more speechlessness, and I'm sure, a few tears from my mom. However, we couldn't deny this was the opportunity I had felt my life led up to. They were able to be part of the whole process, and that was priceless.

I'll never forget the day I talked to my boss at Prestonwood, Matt, a couple of days after I got the call. I'm sure he had a feeling this day was coming eventually, but neither of us had known when. I told him everything that had happened and how I felt this was what I had been born to do.

Matt grew up as a missionary kid, living in El Salvador, so he understood missions and had a heart for reaching other nations and peoples as well. I shared with him how much I loved my job and how I felt bad about leaving the Young Singles women after investing so much.

He told me, "Natalie, leaving this job to follow Jesus overseas and still being single will teach them more than if you were to stay."

That was affirmation and a huge encouragement to me, leaving an amazing job and many of my best friends. Not only was my time at Prestonwood used to teach me how to lead by mentoring women in ministry, but through Matt, I learned how to organize a ministry for street kids. He was a huge instrument God used in teaching me how to lead.

25

I felt God preparing me to move to the Philippines in January of 2013. I had peace in my heart. It was the right timing. I fundraised and left my job at Prestonwood in September of 2012. Fundraising was slow at first, but I knew if God wanted me to move in January, it would all work out.

I updated those who had supported me before on short-term trips. Many knew this would probably happen one day, so it was fun spreading the word.

A mentor helped me research and pray how I would explain to supporters about what exactly God called me to do. Though I had only visited the city where I would live for less than twenty-four hours, God impressed His plans upon me. I knew a good bit about the Philippines at this point, and I prayed God would use me to help the street kids in Cagayan De Oro. I prayed He would go before me and pave the way by preparing the kids, their families, and the community for what God wanted to do. Though I had no experience in this type of ministry, I felt a peace knowing God would be with me along the way. As I shared, I explained to people the vision God had given me.

The fundraising period, from September through December, was a great time of strengthening for me as well as understanding what I was undertaking while I talked with potential supporters. God gave me the chance to speak to several churches and groups and to share my testimony of how God called me from an internship in New York to the streets of the Philippines.

I loved sharing my story with other young girls struggling to discover their meaning in life. Because this ministry was not something I could do without the support of others, I hoped my message encouraged the hearts of many. They were as much a part of this as I was. I have always enjoyed raising awareness and support. Though it wasn't easy, it allowed others to join in and suggested global action.

Regardless of my passion, fundraising was slow. People asked when I was leaving, and I answered, "January 9." Though I didn't have my ticket, I longed to go in January. During December, I stuck with what I felt to be true. Once again, God came through at the right time as if He wanted me to share with as many people as possible and seek Him daily in prayer.

Sometimes, I believe He makes us wait so we will continue to give Him control, knowing that His timing is perfect and His Will will prevail. I received the clearance from K.I.M. to buy my ticket three weeks before my planned departure date. Clearly, He was still answering my prayers and staying true to what I felt Him telling me.

26

My family was so poor we didn't eat at every mealtime. Sometimes root crops were all we ate. My mother was a housewife and a good mother. At least that's what people told me. I can't remember the things she did for me. People said I used to cry like a baby and always wanted my mom. That's normal, I think. My father was a good man, always there for us after our mother died. I remember him combing my hair to look for lice, something my mom used to do.

We lived along a river. If we had no food, we went fishing with my father. One of the many jobs my dad had was making coconut wine. Every day he asked me to take the coconut wine to a store, and I'd get so angry when he asked me to do that. If my classmates saw me, they laughed at me because we didn't have much money. I was already made fun of at school because I didn't have the required school supplies or the nice uniform. I wore flip-flops instead of proper shoes like the rest of them.

Some kids brought their lunches to school, but my food embarrassed me so much that I went home for lunch so they couldn't see what I ate. Usually, my lunch was fried—dried, smelly fish. Every day I climbed the mountain and crossed the river to eat lunch at home. To cross the river, we rode on a bamboo raft and pulled ourselves across with a rope connected to the other side. Sometimes, by the time I got home, there was no food, not even rice. On those days, my father told us to eat bananas.

I remember one time when I asked my mom what we were having for lunch. She said there were bananas in the kitchen. I reminded her that we had bananas for breakfast and dinner the previous night. My father had been gone for several days looking for money, and I was hallucinating and imagining him walking through the door with rice. Miraculously, that day he returned and brought us bread and real food for dinner. It was like a celebration, eating food from the city. Most of the time all we had was fruit grown in the fields around us.

Sometimes, my classmates or my teacher gave me their leftovers if I cleaned up after them. I didn't complain because I knew that was the status of my family. From time to time, I stole fruit from our neighbor to make my stomach stop growling.

My father loved us and wanted to take care of us, but he had only finished second grade. He couldn't get a better job, but he did his best.

God definitely challenged us when my dad passed away. Our life became even more difficult than previously, which I couldn't imagine being possible. It was hard for us to understand as young children that we would be okay again one day.

My older siblings were only a little older than I was and didn't know how to face our reality either or how to care for my younger brother and me. We survived those next few months on root crops, and I'm not sure how that kept us alive.

Every day was hard, and I couldn't understand why God let my parents die. My father's death was the most painful because I was ten years old then and had already lost my mother. After my father died, both my older siblings continued with their own lives, leaving me at home to watch over my little brother. Though I didn't like that, I realized I had taken them for granted when they were home. Soon after, I was separated from all my siblings.

My younger brother was seven when we were separated, and I didn't see him again until he was fifteen. When I finally talked to him, I asked what he had been doing the past years. He seemed burdened by his life choices and too ashamed to tell me.

When I got the chance to visit my siblings, I envisioned we would make new memories together and catch up on lost time. But it didn't happen right away. It was hard to reconnect after eight years apart.

27

On January 9, 2013, at 5 a.m., I said goodbye to my mom and sister and headed to the airport in Jackson, Mississippi, with my dad. We checked in, ate breakfast, and waited until the last minute to say goodbye. I'll never forget what he said to me right before I went through security.

He squeezed me so tight I could barely breathe, and with tears streaming down his face and in a shaky voice, he said, "I'm so proud of you for following what God's called you to do." We both cried.

There was something different in his voice. I've heard my dad say he was proud of me before, but it was for accomplishments like good grades, scoring in a basketball game, or graduating—no small feats. But this felt so much deeper as it was the hardest thing in the world to do—leave everything I knew and love to follow what God had called me to. But, though it hurt him to see me go, he was proud of me. In one moment in that monumental day, there was pain, happiness, joy, and pride.

As hard as it was to leave, in my heart I found peace and comfort, knowing that if I didn't go, no one would. I had the privilege of growing up with a loving family, and I wanted to provide that in some way for the kids of CDO.

K.I.M. believed in helping Christians fulfill their calling; this is another way I found comfort. When I joined, it wasn't about filling a position and doing what I was told. They were a safety net, but it was up to me to follow where God had called me. I was able to be Spirit-led every day, which was necessary in order to know what to do. *This is His ministry, not mine,* I reminded myself. Many times I wondered, *Why me?* I believe it's because I need Him; I'm not qualified. I have to be on my knees daily, prayerfully seeking His wisdom.

When I arrived in the Philippines, I moved to Malaybalay, Bukidnon, a small town in the mountains of Mindanao. Malaybalay was home to approximately 150,000 people, most of whom were commuters or college students of Bukidnon State University, which was about three hours southeast into the mountains behind CDO. Though that seems like many people, the town itself was actually small, with one main grocery store and one outdoor market.

Many people in Malaybalay were farmers, who took advantage of the cooler climate from the mountainous elevation and vast, fertile land. Around just about every corner were rice fields, a necessity for Filipino meals. Several small villages existed in the forest on the outskirts of Malaybalay, where people lived in original Filipino homes of bamboo.

The organization had a children's home there, so I was based near other missionaries while I learned the language and prepared to start the ministry for street kids in CDO. When I arrived in Malaybalay, all of my contacts were, to my surprise, sick and in the hospital. I was already nervous moving to a town I had never visited, and to complicate matters, the people who would have normally greeted me were sick! Not the best start.

I moved in with a young American missionary couple, William and Tara, who were already housing a couple of missionaries from South Africa. The first few months were hard. I thought that it would be easier to adjust being in a town where the organization had a children's home and several full-time missionaries, but for some reason, it wasn't. I didn't feel like myself. I felt lost and out of place as if I didn't belong. I knew, without a doubt, I was supposed to be there. That was a vulnerable season, and Satan knew if he could stop me, that would be the time.

I struggled to feel at home because this wasn't where I'd been called. The organization believed it was best that I learn the language before moving to CDO, and I wanted to respect their authority. I needed to complete this task to reach where God had called me. I needed to learn the language before I could do anything. That was a hard phase—to leave everything and move across the world to help street kids but be unable to do it. I didn't want to give up, but there were times when I thought I might. I studied every waking moment because the harder I worked, the sooner I could do what my heart longed to do.

I was confused why this was so different. In those moments, I wanted to call my parents, my sister or brother, my best friend, or someone else to talk and cry with. However, with the time difference, that was impossible. It was in those times of loneliness that my faith strengthened beyond what it had ever been before. Those times when I wanted my family, I turned to Jesus instead.

Many nights I cried myself to sleep, longing to feel as connected and valuable as I had felt while I lived at Brindy's orphanage. Maybe this is how Brindy felt her first day at the orphanage—alone and out of place. I knew it was wise to learn the language from a distance, but I didn't expect to feel so disconnected from my calling. That season truly deepened my love for Jesus because He comforted me each night. I felt His presence keeping me strong and holding me tight when I was alone.

William and Tara helped me find a tutor; her name was Jonah. She was a student at the local university and taught me as a part-time job. I credit her for all the Visayan I know today. We met for at least five hours each day. When we weren't meeting, I studied, worked on assignments, or practiced what little I knew. Visayan is a local dialect; there was no Rosetta Stone or book to use. It wasn't until halfway through my learning that we finally found a Visayan book that another organization had created. At that point, we used it to review and ensure we had covered everything. With each day, I saw improvements that fueled my desire to stick with it.

28

I have to be honest. As her mom, this was not what I had planned for my daughter. It was "my" dream for her to be on *The Today Show*, broadcasting the news and in the spotlight. I was not happy about it. Of course, I was proud of her heart for Jesus, but I wanted her to do something that would allow her to use that SMU journalism degree. Natalie has always been a driven child, determined to achieve whatever she sets her mind to.

When our family traveled to the Philippines and saw her desire to help the people, I understood why she loved them; they are the sweetest people on earth! But I never imagined she'd go full-time. The short two-week trips were easy for me, but reality hit on July 5, 2012, when we received the call that she'd been accepted to join K.I.M.

I immediately cried and couldn't be excited. Looking back, I think I was one of her biggest obstacles because I tried everything to talk her out of it. It was terrible—I tried to get in the way of God's calling for her life.

Shortly after her fund-raising began, our church and prayer groups prayed for us. I could not be strong and stay focused on the good. I thought about how far Natalie would be from home. What if she needed me, got sick, or was in an accident?

Many times, friends asked me about Natalie being overseas serving in the Philippines, and one friend in particular said, "It's your own damn fault she is over there!"

I couldn't believe she said that to me! Her comment made me think about what she meant. She continued and said that I raised her to care for others and make a difference. It was clear that Natalie understood what was important and that I could learn something from her. Since then I have grown so much as a person, not just as a parent. I have learned how to trust God and put her in His hands.

The most difficult time we said goodbye to Natalie was before her return flight after my son's wedding in the spring of 2013. We knew it would be a long time, possibly a year, before we would see her again. I couldn't breathe leaving the airport, but it helped knowing Brindy needed her. I felt selfish thinking how fortunate we were to miss each other. At least we had a family and would be apart for a short while. Others, like Brindy, are not so blessed.

I had always wanted four children. After our third, life got busy, and we didn't have a fourth. I now realize that God fulfilled this wish for me with Brindy. She is such a blessing to our family and is like a daughter to me. She is my number four!

29

After being at the orphanage for three months and then being home in Mississippi, I felt as if I had abandoned the kids. I knew they were okay and that the Lord would care for them since I didn't feel called to live there at the time, but my heart was heavy. I needed to go back to settle my heart if nothing else.

I decided to surprise the kids by not telling them I would be visiting. When I arrived at the orphanage, the kids were at school. I hid behind the bushes at the entrance of the property where the kids walked home from school. It was so much fun knowing they had no idea I was there. Those were the sweetest embraces because I was able to show them someone loved them enough to keep coming back.

One of the kids signaled that Brindy was coming, and several of them waited around to see her reaction. Of course, she was one of the last to come home that day. When she got close enough, I jumped out at her, causing her to nearly have a heart attack at sixteen. I'm sure tears welled, but she would never admit that.

Those two weeks were necessary for me to find peace after being away while God worked in other ways in my life. It was as if He said to me, "I've got them. You don't have to worry."

I enjoyed spending more time with Brindy. God still had a plan for us, and I was excited to share that with her.

During the trip, she and I had a chance to talk, and I asked, "Do you remember what you wrote when I asked what you wanted to be when you grow up?"

"Yes, I remember," she shyly replied.

"You know, I think God really does have a plan to use us together one day, and I'm excited to see how." I encouraged her and reminded her there'd be something great in our future.

The night before I left, I hung out in the girls' dorm, talking and laughing with them. I gave goodbye hugs, and as I walked away toward the boys' dorm, someone softly called my name. I turned to find Brindy waving through the wood-paneled window of her room.

For the first time ever, she whispered, "I love you."

"I love you, too," I responded as I proceeded to the boys' dorm with a heavy but hopeful heart.

30

Most nights were the same... I prepared for bed after helping the kids with homework, prepared my teaching lesson, or graded papers. Finally, I would turn on the electric fan, turn off the light, unzip the mosquito tent that fit perfectly around the bed, climb in, and stare at the tin roof, reflecting on the day. I prayed for guidance and thanked the Lord for picking me to display love to the kids. I was in awe of how God used the Philippines to shape me.

The sound of the rain on the tin roof, the electric fan, the rustling of rats across the ceiling beams, or the shuffling of little feet were such peaceful sounds as I pondered each day at the orphanage. I dreamed about the future, personally as well as for those children.

How can I do something? What can I do? Who will do it with me? I wondered as I drifted off to sleep.

What seemed like a few hours later, I heard sounds as the boys worked on their chores before breakfast. One of those chores was sweeping the entire orphanage grounds to clear the paths of fallen leaves from the overnight rain. Along with the sweeping of leaves, came sounds of rushing water when the boys took bucket showers.

Every now and then, if one of the kids got enough sleep, I heard singing during chores and shower time. Precious noises I would always cherish but that never got me out of bed until I heard the breakfast bell. I guess you could say 4 a.m. isn't my style!

That season of my life, I grew closer to the Lord and learned to talk with Him about everything. I knew He would answer those dreams in His way and in His time.

31

The thought of Natalie living overseas was overwhelming. As her father, I was afraid someone would take advantage of my little darling and I'd be helpless if she were ever to get hurt. We are a close-knit family, and I always enjoyed watching her mom lead her through life to become a woman.

It would be difficult for my wife, Angela, not to participate closely in Natalie's daily life while Natalie navigated through this next chapter. However, I was proud she was doing God's work and that she cared so much about the souls of lost people, people who are seen by many as unworthy, third-world beings. Natalie had always been steadfast and driven, and I had no doubt she would be successful in establishing a ministry for street kids. I was inspired and eager to watch her calling unfold and see what God would do through her. I felt a sense of pride to have contributed to her life's development and knew she could survive without me.

I did not see Natalie becoming a missionary, but it wasn't completely farfetched. She had been on a path to become a journalist and could easily work on special assignments overseas. She had a big heart for others, so I knew she would somehow incorporate that in her life.

Natalie has always had a sense of purpose to excel in school and develop skills for an exciting life and career, with curiosity and enjoyment along the way. I knew God had unique plans for her after her brush with death as a young child.

When she was two years old, her mother and I went away for the weekend, each in different directions. I was on my way to a fishing trip with my dad while she was staying with my mother, who was, and still is, called "Mamaw."

Natalie and her cousins were at Mamaw's house. While the cousins swam, Natalie removed her "floaties" and played on the swing set. When she decided to swim again, she forgot to put on her "floaties" and slipped into the pool without anyone noticing. Soon after, Mamaw and her aunt Suzanne, my sister, saw Natalie on the bottom of the pool. Immediately, they called 9-1-1, dove in, and administered CPR. They reached her just in time.

I was already on my way to the Gulf Coast to meet my dad on his boat that we all loved so much. However, while en route to the coast, my uncle called and said I needed to return home. Natalie was in the hospital. He immediately said she was all right, but I should be with her and Angela. I've never felt so alone as I did while I drove back to the hospital, constantly praying she had not been underwater too long and would not be subject to brain damage.

When I arrived at the hospital, Angela met me outside crying but said Natalie would be okay. We immediately went to her side, finding her awake but with a sad face as though she had disappointed us in some way. I smiled at her, hugged her the best I could, and told her I loved her while reassuring her all would be okay. She smiled and appeared happy I was there.

We were thankful and knew God had a plan for her life. We had no idea what that plan would be and how she would be used by Him.

Natalie, without being pushed, had always been deeply involved in school and church activities. She was inquisitive about local, state, and world affairs when in school.

Natalie's namesake was a dear college friend of mine and Angela's who worked as a journalist at CNN. When Natalie got to SMU and took a keen interest in journalism, it became clearer that this was her space and her purpose, engaging in worldly activities and living in the visible space of everyday life, locally and around the world. I envisioned her working at a news station or presenting special documentaries on interesting subjects.

In 2010, her life took a turn when she went on a mission trip that changed the trajectory of her life. Later, when I took her to the airport in 2013, I knew that it was a monumental day for the both of us. I was overcome with emotions of pride that my child was truly faithful to God and aspired to make an eternal difference by sharing Jesus with people, young and old, particularly those who were rarely valued by the world.

I was also deeply saddened that I wouldn't be able to give her a hug when she was scared or excited about an achievement. I would miss those opportunities to laugh with her, joke with her, eat with her, cook with her, celebrate birthdays together, be together as a complete family, and participate in the daily things we take for granted when we are on the same side of the planet.

Another part of me envied her. She had the courage to go into an unknown world, trusting God at a level I had never reached. Yet I found relief, knowing my little darling followed the Lord and would never waver from Him. I felt she was prepared to handle the various environments and situations she'd likely never experienced before; she was certainly confident and bright enough to figure things out.

It has been encouraging to watch her plans unfold over the years. Fortunately, she lets me be a part of the ministry and calls often for advice, and I am eager to see what is next on this journey.

32

In March of 2013, I went home for my brother's wedding. Many people thought I should have waited until after his wedding to move to the Philippines, but I'm glad it worked out the way it did because that break came at the perfect time. I desperately needed encouragement from loved ones and a break to renew my spirit.

People were afraid if I went home that soon that I wouldn't return because it was in the middle of the hardest stage of moving overseas. For me, it's not about not wanting to push through; it's about not feeling stuck in the Philippines. That's one thing I have learned that is essential to ministry, at least for me—the freedom to be myself and continue a life at home as well.

My family and I are so close that I could not sign a contract or do anything that would keep me from being apart from the important events in life. I have met missionaries who signed a twenty-five year contract. I'm not saying that's wrong, but it's not for me. I may be a missionary for twenty-five or thirty years, even longer, but I would struggle making a big decision at such an early stage in my life.

I'm leery of planning too much. I do believe God can reveal to someone that he or she is supposed to commit to twenty-five years. God has revealed things very clearly to me before, so I understand that. But that wasn't a call He had given to me. Throughout my story, God gives me tasks, missions, or projects to complete instead of timeframes. I use my ability to commit as a sign of devotion to the project, program, or mission He has laid before me.

When I returned home for my brother's wedding, I was tired, discouraged, and down, but that didn't affect my determination to do what God had called me to. It simply was time for me to be refreshed.

Of course, I was going to return to the Philippines, but I would be lying if I told you it was easy. It was harder than the first time I left because I was going back to something I knew felt impossible when I was there. There were far more tears leaving this time than the last.

33

After my brother's wedding, I found my seat on the plane and tried to hold myself together. A young girl about my age sat next to me. She wore a bracelet with the Lord's Prayer written on it. Through my sadness, I mentioned that I loved her bracelet, and we began talking.

Talking to her helped me focus on my calling and not my emotions at the time. If it weren't for her, I probably would have cried the entire flight. She was a teacher, so we had a great conversation about our kids. At the end of the flight, she turned to me, took off her bracelet, and said, "Here, you take it, and I hope it encourages you in your ministry." I was so touched by such a simple act.

Gestures like those mean the world to me and have encouraged me on this journey. I hope someday she knows how big a role she played that day.

Honestly, I don't know if I'd have gotten on the plane to go back if it hadn't been for Brindy. She was my motivation. After the plane landed, I went straight to the orphanage where Brindy grew up to see her graduate from her first two years of college.

Arriving at the orphanage was a breath of fresh air. It was wonderful to see the Philippines I knew and loved. Brindy knew I wasn't just in town to see her graduate. She had agreed to move with me to Malaybalay and help me start the ministry for street kids in CDO. It was the beginning of a new and exciting journey for us both. Our work would be her first glimpse of ministry and life outside of the orphanage, which would be very different from the sheltered environment she had lived in for over six years.

What I felt God calling me toward became clearer when I learned what Brindy would have done after graduation if it hadn't been for me. She would have gone to live with her uncle and looked for a job. There is no way to know what her life would have looked like, but it would have been very different from where she is now. God gave me a vision of the impact she could create by helping kids like herself, but I knew she needed a little encouragement along the way that she may not have gotten had she not come with me.

At graduation, the students' parents escorted them down the aisle to their seats. A couple of the houseparents were with us at the graduation, but Brindy asked me to escort her. I was honored, and it was one of the first outward symbols that we were family.

A few days after graduation, we began our journey together in a motorela, which is a passenger cart connected to a motorcycle. She kept laughing and saying she thought she was dreaming, that this wasn't really happening. It was just as surreal to me.

34

And so Brindy's and my journey began...

In order to reach Malaybalay, we had to fly through Manila, the capital of the Philippines, or take a fifteen-hour bus ride. Since Brindy had never been to Manila nor flown on an airplane, we decided the plane would be more fun. She used the airplane lavatory for the first time—I made her go even though she didn't need to. She said she jumped back and yelled when she pushed the flush button. Everything was new; I even had to help her fasten her seatbelt. When the flight attendants explained what happened if we experienced a loss of cabin pressure, she was clearly nervous. I told her not to worry, that I would put on my mask first and then assist her.

The first day we were in Manila, we went to the mall to see a movie. We needed a break from the Manila heat, and she had never been to a movie theater. When we arrived, the only movie showing was in 3D, something else she'd never experienced, and she wanted to keep the glasses. After the movie, we found a Dairy Queen, and Brindy ate her first Blizzard ever. She was amazed when they turned the milkshake upside down and it didn't fall out; she tried to catch it!

This was also her first time to see another orphanage. Manila is home to the headquarters for K.I.M., including an orphanage, a school, a birthing clinic, a dental clinic, a home for girls, and more. She got a good idea of what a ministry could become with lots of prayer and hard work. I wanted her to know what was there and to be inspired to help me take our ministry to as many people as possible. She was my insider to the culture of children's homes and the emotions of feeling neglected or abandoned, and I was preparing her to be ready for the kids we would help.

When Brindy and I arrived in Malaybalay, we transferred to another house that she and I would share, so the surroundings were new to both of us. When we walked in, she began exploring.

She said, "This is *my* room?" She had never had her own room before, and she was beyond excited. It felt so good to give that to her though she was a bit overwhelmed.

The first night, she stayed in my room because we didn't have a bed for her. Later that week, we bought furniture, a refrigerator, and a stove, and we settled in.

Brindy was painfully shy. Filipino culture is generally more reserved, but she was beyond that. I'd invite people over to our new house, and she would let me introduce her and then disappear into her room. I knew it was a big adjustment, so I left her alone. I tried to be as positive as I could be while she settled in so she would feel at home with me.

Brindy knew a little English, and I knew a little Ilonggo—her language. However, we both needed to learn Visayan, the language of Malaybalay and CDO. I knew the basics at this point, and she could understand me but would respond in her own dialect. It created a lot of confusion as well as laughter when we struggled to connect in a mutual language. We bonded over things that didn't cause a language barrier: food and our puppy.

This was the beginning of a new season for us and a journey of healing for Brindy that we weren't aware needed to happen.

35

I had battles and difficult times with Natalie, a battle between my heart and my brain when we lived together in Malaybalay. Every day something happened—good and bad. That's when my trials began, and I was the only one who knew it. Sometimes my heart and my head would fight. There were situations when I would stop talking and shut down. Even if I knew Natalie was joking, it felt like a big stab in the back because I didn't understand. I never told Natalie what the problem was, and I could not tell her my feelings for the longest time.

It wasn't easy living with an American girl. We came from different worlds and different situations. Everything was different, but I knew God connected us. I had nowhere else to go, so I stayed.

We lived in a big house, the first time I ever lived in a concrete house. My other homes were constructed of bamboo or coconut lumber. I was so happy and confident that this was it—the life I dreamed of. However, sometimes Satan tried to keep me from enjoying myself, as if I had a battle within me every single day. I thought I had recovered from the past, but sadly, everything came back after leaving the orphanage. That was the first time in years I felt alone again—when I moved in with Natalie. I felt I wasn't good enough to stay with her.

I came from the poorest family and didn't know what to do or how to act with her. I was full of hatred and angry with my family, my relatives, and God. No one had taken care of me, visited, or contacted me while I was in the orphanage, which was why I was scared to love and trust people again. It was difficult, and I was afraid anyone I let in would do the same to me as my family had—leave.

Yes, I loved "Ate" Natalie, but I couldn't show her I loved her because I didn't know what to do. It was hard to trust her and share my life with her, and that's why we fought. She wanted to be a part of my life, but my heart would not open, as if it was wired shut. Since the beginning, she'd always encouraged me and never stopped loving me. I might have been able to open up one day, but until then my heart was trapped.

36

Brindy coming into my home was a huge leap of faith. I didn't have a background in childcare or experience with parenting, and I didn't know this would be as big a challenge or calling as it turned out to be. I had a strong bond with Brindy, and sending her back to live with relatives who could not care for her was not an option. I thought we would be friends and roommates, and I would be a mentor and big sister. I assumed her living with me would be a mere stepping-stone toward giving her the chance to break the cycle of poverty that entangled her family.

From the outside, Brindy was the luckiest orphan in the world. She had everything imaginable at her fingertips. Most importantly, she had a support system in me that would stand by her no matter what.

It didn't take long to notice that mountains of information and emotion were hidden inside her, but she wouldn't let me in. It would take time for us to become comfortable with one another, but I realized it wasn't just that she was uncomfortable. On the inside, she was in agony.

This was the first time in Brindy's life she had to face the reality of situations that had shaped her. Whether she liked it or not, this was her life, and she needed to choose whether it would consume her or make her stronger. She was much more alive at night, and those were the fun times. When we laughed, everything was okay.

We cooked together, cleaned together, and watched movies almost every night. A few weeks in, it was almost as if a cloud came upon her when I went to my room each night. A pattern evolved, and I stayed up later to observe more.

It wasn't long before I asked questions. I was concerned about what was bothering her. She wasn't handling the situation well. I thought time would help her adjust, but this was much deeper. I let her know I was there if she needed to talk. Normally, that would open the door by ensuring there was someone who would listen.

Oh, if I could count the number of nights when her answer to "what's wrong?" was "nothing." I let it go in the beginning because I didn't want to force her to talk. Then I realized she needed to talk and ignoring her feelings would never bring healing.

The first few attempts were not very successful... Before long, she knew my questions were coming and would brush me off and say "Goodnight" before I could ask. She would quickly run to her room and lock the door. I wanted so badly to be there for her, but she wouldn't let me. Often, I heard her crying in her room, and I was dumbfounded. *What could possibly be wrong?*

The first time she cried in front of me felt like a major breakthrough. That was the first time she let me comfort her. Then, there was the first time she yelled at me when she got mad. Progress! She shared how she felt she wasn't good enough or wasn't equal. She felt lesser than I was, and no matter what I said, she shut down and wouldn't let me pick her back up.

Many times our arguments were misunderstandings, but there was no room to explain and straighten things out until days later. She was good at the silent treatment, a powerful defense mechanism that ended up hurting her more than me. However, it was painful to watch her punish herself that way.

She continually said, "I don't want to be a burden."

"But not talking is hurting us both more than if you would just tell me what is bothering you," I suggested.

Over time, it weighed on me because I carried her happiness on my shoulders. I had to learn the hard way that parenting is tough—so tough! Here I was, twenty-five years old with an eighteen-year-old... I know that sounds strange, but Brindy hadn't had the chance to grow up as I had. Emotionally, she was about twelve years old, the age when she arrived at the orphanage. She had stopped growing emotionally, pushed aside her feelings, and ignored what went on inside of her.

I realize not all kids have the same story, and this is not to say the orphanage didn't nurture her, because it did. The houseparents loved her, cared for her, provided her with a family environment, educated her, and introduced her to Jesus. However, many people who have been through trauma tend to close themselves off from others or create a shell and keep their feelings inside.

Brindy was one of those. I had to help her remove the shell she created in order to address the issues inside of her to avoid further trauma. Brindy was good at hiding things. Most people had no idea how she truly felt.

Naturally, the moment Brindy was alone with her thoughts, away from others who had similar stories, it all but suffocated her. There were times that all I could do was sit back and watch, praying for relief, understanding, and for God to free her from this bondage.

One day, Brindy said she obtained her sister's phone number, and I encouraged her to call. She was hesitant because she was hurt her family hadn't tried to contact her for several years.

"Maybe they didn't know how to contact you or that it was okay to visit you," I said as I tried to comfort her.

37

After leaving the orphanage, I lived in Malaybalay with Natalie. I had not spoken with my siblings since I was ten, so they didn't know I'd been discharged from the orphanage or that I'd been living with someone and would one day work in Cagayan De Oro. One of my relatives gave me the contact number for my family through Facebook. The first time I saw it, I didn't think I should call and wanted to ignore or delete the message. A part of me didn't care, but Natalie encouraged me to communicate with my brothers and sisters.

At that time, it was August, my birthday month, and my father's death anniversary was coming up on November 15. Natalie told me this would be the right time to communicate with them.

I decided to call, but when I was dialing the number, I kept erasing it. I was so scared they would ignore my call or wouldn't know me. My hands shook the entire time, and my heart thumped.

Finally, I called. Immediately, somebody answered the phone, but I hung up. I called again, and someone answered again. I didn't know if it was my brother or my sister. I had no idea whose number I was calling but assumed it was my sister.

She said, "Who is this, please?"

I said, "Hi, my name is Brindy."

She replied, "Oh, where did you get my number? Where are you now?"

"I'm in Malaybalay, living with someone who is taking good care of me." That was all I said.

I wondered why they weren't happier I had called... I didn't finish our conversation; I just hung up.

Months went by, and I didn't contact them. Though they texted me, I didn't reply. In November, I decided to communicate because I wanted to honor the death anniversary of my father and see them after eight years. We talked again and planned when I would visit and where I'd stay.

That telephone call gave me a glimpse of what my siblings sounded like. For years, I hadn't heard their voices. I had no idea what they looked like. I needed to see them and forgive them for not visiting or communicating with me all those years. I reminded myself that life was unfair. It wasn't their decision that the three of them lived together and I was sent somewhere else. But it still hurt.

I'm happy they didn't ignore my phone call. That conversation changed everything, and my visit to their homes opened my eyes to understand how God could use what had happened to me for the good.

38

Manny Pacquiao was a street kid who became one of the world's greatest boxers of all time. Pacquiao's story demonstrates that every kid is capable of reaching success, however they may define that, or breaking the cycle of poverty. Many street kids are children of street kids; it's a vicious cycle. All they need is a chance, an opportunity to allow them the choice of stepping out of that cycle. Pacquiao was given a chance. Someone saw potential in him. Potential can be found in every child, but they need someone to help them see it.

Pacquiao exemplifies a life that Christ can redeem. He once lost himself through his fame to alcohol and gambling. Eventually, he found Christ, turned from his old ways, and proclaimed Jesus as his Savior and Lord.

I'm always brought back to a verse in Psalm 86:11: "Teach me Your way, O Lord, that I may walk in Your truth." He can't do that unless I first come to Him, ask Him, and listen. I have to be teachable.

Part of the beauty of following Jesus is that He requires all that is within us and then takes us places we could never go on our own. Without prayer, I wouldn't be where I am today; I would have taken a different path. However, not too long ago, I began praying that verse over and over. And each time I prayed, I was on my knees before the Lord, begging Him to show me *His* way because I was tired of *my* way.

The truth was, I asked Him to teach me His way because I didn't have a way. I didn't know how to meet the needs of hundreds of thousands of kids on the street in the Philippines. I didn't know how to meet Brindy's needs, either. So I turned to my Teacher, who fed thousands with only five fish and seven loaves of bread (Matthew 15:36). When I think about that, I know that with Him I can do this. His Holy Spirit lives within me. In the same way that He fed those thousands, feeding hundreds of street kids is easy for Him. I just had to be teachable and let Him.

That's been my prayer for a while now, and it continues to be. I'll always want to know His way over mine, and I'm daily seeking that in our ministry.

Pacquiao spoke at a rally I attended in CDO and shared, "All of my trophies will be nothing in Heaven. All that matters is that I know Jesus."

The kids in our ministry were there that day, and I hope they heard the depth in that statement and saw there was hope for their future even beyond this world. They can be like Pacquiao if given a chance.

39

Because I couldn't take all of the kids from Uncle Dick's Home on a trip to America, I decided I would bring America to them. What better way than through food? I wanted them to know what Southern food tasted like so they could experience a little of how I grew up.

The kids already wondered why I was so weird, eating cereal or toast and eggs for breakfast. It was such a foreign idea for them, watching what I was served each meal.

"Where is your rice?" they asked.

To show them, we set a date for "American Day." American Day was to be an entire day when the kids would eat only the American food I prepared for them and what was sure to be a shock for the kids—no rice! I prepared the menu and woke up early that Saturday morning to make blueberry pancakes from scratch and chocolate milk for sixty people.

The kids were worried they wouldn't survive a whole day without rice. They enjoyed the pancakes, but felt as if they were eating dessert for breakfast. A couple of hours after breakfast was "merienda" (or snack time, as Americans call it), when I served pineapple icebox pie. I could only serve the pie frozen because of the lack of ingredients in the local market, which ruined the consistency. I had wanted to make a lemon icebox pie from Mamaw's recipe, but finding lemons is like finding gold in the southern Philippines.

Our lunch was, of course, a great all-American burger. My cooking helpers were shocked I didn't mix anything into the uncooked hamburger meat to make it stretch for all sixty people; this was a true burger. We also made homemade garlic French fries—a personal first for me, actually slicing and frying the potatoes. The course was served with a side of local watermelon. There were no leftovers.

We spent the entire afternoon preparing a Mississippi favorite: fried catfish dinner, complete with homemade mac and cheese and (drumroll, please!) hushpuppies made from scratch.

I didn't know they had catfish in the Philippines, but they did.

The best part was how accurate my request for fresh catfish was. The fish arrived from the market in a blue cellophane bag. We carried the bag to the sink to clean and prepare the fish for fillets and when I opened the bag, they came out swimming. I screamed and leaped backward while the kids burst into laughter. They'd known the fish were alive and wanted to see how funny it would be to scare me. I was horrified. Some of the kids prepared the fish while I recovered from my shock. These sure were the freshest fish I had ever cooked!

After dinner, I had a surprise for them. Some of the older boys built a bonfire, and I introduced my personal favorite and a must-try for all kids—s'mores. It didn't take long for them to figure it out. We laughed as marshmallows were burned to a crisp and sticky fingers were like suckers once the last marshmallow was roasted. We had so much fun, and that became our tradition. After that, every time I visited, I made sure to request a s'mores night.

40

"**W**hat time will y'all be awake and ready to go tomorrow?" I asked. We had organized a trip to the swimming pool with the street kids we were getting to know in Malaybalay. This was guaranteed to be a special day for the kids who didn't get many fun surprises.

Brindy and I planned this in the midst of my learning the language, which was another way for me to practice my language skills as we prepared for the ministry we intended to launch.

"8 a.m.," they replied.

These kids didn't get up that early, which most likely meant they were planning to stay up all night eagerly awaiting our adventure.

We met them at Jollibee, a Filipino fast food restaurant where many street kids go to beg for food, and about nine street boys piled in my car, wide-eyed and excited for the day. It wasn't hard to entertain them. They had never been in a car and wanted the whole town to see how special they were as they waved at everyone we passed by.

One of their favorite games of the day was catching a Frisbee in the air just before splashing into the pool. I couldn't count the number of action pictures we snapped that day nor the races to see who was the fastest swimmer.

Before lunch, I gathered them to share the Gospel, which they had already heard from different mission groups over the years. We learned many of the kids hadn't accepted Him as their Savior until someone showed them the love of Christ through building a relationship with them beyond simply telling His story. They were each receptive, insinuating they were closer to making the decision to follow Christ.

We had enough food to fill their bellies and send them home with a plate for later. I became quite the expert at making Filipino spaghetti, which consisted of spaghetti noodles, sweet tomato sauce, cream, and a topping of sliced hotdogs. I also learned to make macaroni salad: a mixture of macaroni noodles, cream, condensed milk, mixed fruit cocktail, and coconut jellies. Let me know if you would like me to cater your next party!

The boys had so much fun getting to be kids. That wasn't an everyday feeling for them, having someone provide their immediate needs, and we got to do more of that: providing a place for them to just have fun.

There was one little guy in particular, Jay, who was precious. He was new; I hadn't seen him before. We hit it off right away. Everyone had a spare change of clothes except for him. So he decided to swim nude in the public pool! Good thing he was young enough that it was acceptable.

When he was tired of swimming, he was freezing. I gave him my towel, and he and his brother sat in the sun with it. They were so proud to have the towel that they kept waving at me whenever I checked on them.

At the end of the day, we gathered our things to head back, and the bigger boys took the heavy stuff for me. My little man Jay came straight for my hand.

To get to the car, we had to walk up a steep, muddy hill, and little Jay didn't have any shoes. I carried him up the hill, and he grinned and smiled all the way. I prayed we wouldn't slip and fall!

That group of boys lived in the back of the Jollibee parking lot and showered and drank from the restaurant's water hose. This particular day, they experienced not needing to worry about where they would drink or bathe or even eat. They knew then how much we truly cared for them, and that Jesus was the reason. As we drove away, I high-fived everyone and little Jay pulled my hand toward him and gave me a kiss.

Street kids are so sweet—they really are. They need time, love, and care to see past their "survival skills," which many people see as the bad things they do. *Do you blame them?* I would probably steal, too, if I was starving and had no money to buy anything. That's when I decided to do something about it. I wanted to love them through their "decisions" and slowly prove to them that they don't need to make those decisions anymore. We had to show them that God doesn't forget about His children, even when their earthly fathers and mothers abandon them or fail to provide for them.

God never will.

41

"**W**ill you please tell me what's wrong? You know I love you, and I just want you to be happy," I begged.

Brindy and I must have been going back and forth for over an hour. It was a cycle of asking, encouraging and waiting for a reply. I just wanted her to open up.

She began to see how her silence hurt me and said, "Why did this happen only to me?"

Though Brindy wasn't alone in her pain, she was the only one of her siblings who was taken away. The rest of them stayed together with a relative near where they had grown up. So naturally she wondered, *Why me? Why couldn't I stay with them, too?*

It was easier for me to see how God could bring good from this. She had been separated and sent away, cutting her deeply, making her feel unwanted and like an outcast from her family.

During the time she battled with this, she couldn't see how her path, whether she had chosen it or not, was the better path. Her journey was set apart for something remarkable. She was chosen by God to be used by Him, and she couldn't see that her life was special, that she was meant for something more.

I encouraged her to visit her siblings to reconnect but also to see what her life would have been like had she not been taken to the orphanage. This trip was eye opening for her, allowing her to realize that *just maybe* her path was the best thing that could have happened to her.

42

November 10, 2013, the week of the anniversary of my father's death, I decided to visit my hometown. It had been more than eight years since I had seen my siblings. Before that I had no plans to visit them, and I didn't know why.

I contacted my younger brother. I told him I was coming home, asked his boss to give him a little time off to spend with his family, and looked toward the five days we would have together. We had nowhere to stay, so my brother called my sister and asked to stay at her house. Everything was set.

I was overwhelmed and anxious about going home.

After eight hours of travel, I met my brother.

The last time we had seen each other, he was so little. This time, he was taller than I was. I hugged him, and said, "How are you?"

We rode a bus for four more hours, and I asked what his reaction had been when he first saw me.

He said, "I thought you were a nun."

He thought that because I grew up in the orphanage and assumed nuns had taken care of me.

We finally arrived, and my sister was waiting for us. When she saw me, she cried and hugged me. I didn't do anything but asked, "How are you?"

Inside, I had hatred toward them. I was the black sheep of the family. During the five days I stayed with them, I saw the closeness between them. Sometimes they talked about memories that didn't include me, as if there were only three of them in the family.

I cried many times and wondered why I didn't belong with them. I tried to think about the good things they remembered about me.

Over the years, they hadn't visited or contacted me, but I told myself to build new memories. They lived with nothing and longed for the love of our parents. I knew my siblings had heartaches but they had moved on in life because they were together.

The things I learned when I visited my siblings were important, and I am thankful I visited them. Together, we remembered the death anniversary of our father, an event that helped us remember we were one; we were family and God hadn't left us. My siblings had grown so much, especially my older brother. He had a family of his own, as did my sister.

I was not the only one who'd been hurt, but each of us had a purpose in this world. We couldn't change our lives, but we could use our lives for God.

Today, my relationships with my brothers and sister are much better. I finally opened my heart again to give them a chance to be my siblings. I have been healed by the love of God and the people around me.

43

It was a typical afternoon playing "Jack Stone," also known as "jacks," at Uncle Dick's Home. I had never played before since the game was more popular in my dad and grandfather's time, but the kids loved playing against me because they would always win.

I was with the girls in their dorm above the dining area when a beautiful beam of sunset burst through the doorway of the second-floor entrance. "Wow! Look at the sunset." Before I could finish my sentence, the twins, Maril and Marice, jumped up and ran to stand in the doorway, facing me.

"What are you doing?" I asked, as they weren't looking at the beautiful site.

They quickly replied, "We're blocking the sun from your skin."

Everyone wants what he or she doesn't have. I look at Filipinos and see beautiful, dark features and a skin color I long for. They look at me and see my white skin, and they use whitening soap in hopes of attaining that. That was when we had our first discussion about skin color and their beauty.

As I laughed at their gesture, I realized they believed my skin color made me more beautiful than them. I always told them how beautiful they were, and many times, one would reply, "No, I'm ugly." I insisted they know their beauty and that God made them just the way they were. There was only one Maril and one

Marice. Yes, they were twins, but they were each unique and completely special in God's eyes.

It was interesting to hear they knew what they wanted to look like but didn't know who they wanted to become. When I asked the kids in the orphanage what they wanted to be when they grew up, they didn't know. I believe their past keeps them from believing in themselves. Because they grew up in an orphanage, they believe they are not capable of what other kids with families are capable of. They feel less valued in society, and I have seen that manifest itself in the simplest of ways. They believe if they looked different, their life would be different.

44

Just like many girls growing up, I always desired to marry and have a family. Maybe because I wanted that so much, I was too committed in every relationship. I didn't have many relationships since one of them lasted seven and a half years.

After that relationship, I didn't want to date anyone else until I found someone with similar passions and dreams. I knew if God was calling me to the Philippines, He would have to place that on someone else's heart as well. I never doubted God would provide a husband for me, but I prayed earnestly because I wanted to be in tune with what God was trying to show me while focusing on the task.

While preparing to move to the Philippines, Satan started attacking me. He was determined to use anything and everything to prevent me from going. He even used what people I knew and loved would say to try to discourage me.

At first, because I was single, I was hesitant when God called me to the Philippines. I thought for sure I would marry before leaving.

In my season of fundraising and preparing, I met guys, but when I told them what I was doing, they applauded my bravery and showed no more interest. Many of them said I was such a good person. They didn't get it.

I'm not a good person. I'm a sinner. I have failed in many areas, including the time when I put a boyfriend and my career path before the Lord. I am a servant. This life is not my own. During this season, I adopted my life verse of Acts 20:24: "But my life is worth nothing to me unless I use it to finish the work assigned me by the Lord Jesus—to share the Good News of the Gospel of Jesus Christ."

People who loved me said things like:

"Are you sure you want to move there?"

"Why not just visit each summer?"

"You're going to give up an opportunity at *The Today Show*?"

"You will never get married."

"Wow, that's amazing you are giving up marriage."

"Everyone will forget about you."

"You will miss out on so much!"

My God is big. He has plans beyond anything we could ever imagine, and I chose to trust that His ways are best regardless of the opinions of others. Even if some of those statements became true, God would be in control and sovereign over that.

While I was in the Philippines for three months in 2010, I prayed often for God to bring someone to work alongside me. I needed a partner and encourager, as did the kids who needed to see a father figure who loved Jesus as well.

Many times during those prayers, God whispered Daniel's name to me. However, I simply thought, *Oh, there's no way! How would that work out?* I always assumed I would meet my husband, from a very different background, later in life. But it felt like a specific Daniel—someone I had grown up with. We hadn't even dated; we were just friends.

The season before I moved, most guys weren't interested because that would be crazy; I was moving to Asia! I prayed during that time that God would protect my heart from anyone who distracted me from my calling.

I was amazed God so clearly answered that prayer. Though that was hard, I was thankful.

45

When I was in middle school, while on Christmas break, I was on a youth trip with my church in Tennessee. We were leaving an indoor skiing facility when I noticed we were missing a large red, puffy jacket. That's what he was wearing. Our leaders assumed everyone was accounted for, but for some reason I was the only one who realized the "red jacket" was missing.

That's when I started noticing him. There was something about him. But we were young, and he was younger than I was, which I thought was not cool in middle school and high school. It was nearly impossible for Daniel and me to have a chance.

If you ask him, he was always looking for a window in. There weren't many opportunities for him to swoop in during my seven-year relationship with someone else, but he found ways to place himself in my life and took a seat as one of my best friends. We saw each other every Tuesday night at Praise Team worship practice, and afterward we both lingered, hoping to talk to one another. After practice one night, when I had briefly broken up with my boyfriend, I almost openly told him I was interested so he would make a move. He assumed because I was older, *by nine months*, that I was "out of his league" so he didn't say anything.

I'll never forget the first time I heard him sing... He sang "The Voice of Truth" by Casting Crowns at church.

No one even knew he could sing, especially not like that, and I was captivated. We remained friends, but a relationship never seemed to work out. Shortly after that, I got back together with my boyfriend.

In 2005, hurricane Katrina hit Mississippi, and though my hometown, Magee, was approximately 200 miles off the coast, we lost power, water, and many trees. Daniel and his mom called the next day to make sure we were okay. *They don't normally call...* I'm sure he was worried. The whole community came together the next day to help remove trees from homes, provide food, etc.

Daniel and I, and a few other friends, formed a group to help people clean. At the time, I had taken another break from the other guy, so Daniel had a chance to ask me on a date. He drove me to Jackson, the nearest city with power, and took me to dinner. *He was so nervous.*

Not long after that, we went on a second date but that was after he had torn his ACL, MCL, and PCL while playing football. During that time, I tried to show him I was interested. I brought cookies and coffee to him after his surgery. Our feelings for each other were always there, but we were afraid the other didn't reciprocate.

One morning in 2012, while I was running, I prayed my same prayer that God would continue to protect me from anyone and anything that would distract me from moving to the Philippines. This particular morning, I remember vividly and earnestly reciting that prayer.

That evening, I went to see Daniel lead worship at his church. He had been leading there for almost a year, and since I was in Texas, working at Prestonwood, I hadn't visited yet. I was shocked at what a great worship leader he was. That was the first time I had seen him use his gifts to the fullest.

Later, we went to Leatha's Bar-B-Que Inn in Hattiesburg, for amazing Mississippi barbeque. There were several of us, and we enjoyed catching up. Everyone could tell that Daniel and I had a connection, but we'd been friends for so long it seemed natural to stay friends.

Anna, my brother's fiancée at the time, told my college roommate Natalie, "Why don't they just date? They clearly like each other."

On the drive home, I couldn't stop thinking about him. I prayed, "Lord, why are you not protecting my heart from him? He has a great job here and is doing what he wants to do. This could never work out. Why do I feel this way?"

An overwhelming sense of fear was drowning me. *What if he is the one and I never give him a chance? I don't want to live without fully knowing.*

I tried so hard to brush off my feelings. I couldn't sleep that night. Never before has anything in my life kept me from sleeping—something was definitely going on inside of me.

My friend Natalie was staying with me. I was glad she woke up to use the restroom in the middle of the night because I needed to talk. "Natalie, I can't sleep. What if he's the one?"

I cried while sharing my fear about never giving him a chance. I told her about my prayer and how God had been answering by keeping guys away and protecting my heart, but He did not keep me from feeling something for Daniel this time. I couldn't ignore that.

She agreed we needed to pray about it and see how I felt after a few days. I had a trip planned for Texas to visit my friends again before moving to the Philippines. While there, I talked with mentors Lainie and Debbie about my feelings and how to deal with them. They agreed I shouldn't start something that would hinder my work in the Philippines, which was so clearly from God.

They advised me to pray and wait to see if God put the same thing on Daniel's heart because he needed to be the one to share his feelings first.

A few weeks later, Daniel invited me to his house, and I said I'd bring a pecan pie because that was his favorite and mine were "the best." He replied he was more excited for me to be there than to get the pie. That gave me the idea he was planning to say something.

That night, we talked, laughed, and ate pie. He finally said, "I don't know how this will work with you in the Philippines; but I really like you, and I want to try."

Grinning ear to ear, I didn't know what to say, but my heart was about to burst. He'd taken a leap of faith, not knowing how I felt. He knew this was his last opportunity before he lost me across the ocean.

We decided to keep in touch and see what happened. Unfortunately, it didn't take long for him to get cold feet. Within the first week of moving to the Philippines, he rarely responded to me. It had been tremendously difficult to move across the ocean, and for him to stop talking to me was horrific.

After four days in the Philippines, my mom called to tell me that Pop, my grandfather, had passed away. On top of moving and being away from family, my heart ached that I could not be with my mom during that time. And with Daniel not talking to me, it was extra hard.

When I left home, I knew I would probably not see Pop again. We had a great visit, and he told me how proud he was and how much he loved me. Every time I visited him, he always asked if I had found someone to take care of me. When I said no, he replied with such confidence and a sweet half-smile, "You will."

46

My life was miserable when God took away my parents. Sometimes when I talked to God I asked, "Why, why, why did you take our parents so early, and why did you do this to me? Why did you leave me in this world? Why do I need to be far from my family?"

Sometimes, I wished I wasn't in this world so I couldn't feel hatred, emptiness, loss, and pain. I hated my life. I hated being in this world.

I was jealous of those children who had parents. I was reminded of that every day when I saw parents walking their kids to school. I cried even though I tried to ignore it and look the other way.

I was angry at the world in general and even at Natalie. I envied her because she had everything in her life and never experienced what I'd been through. Sometimes, because of that, even if she asked me what was wrong, I didn't talk to her. I couldn't look in her eyes because I was afraid she'd figure out that I envied her. I was so sensitive to her words and actions.

I was like that because no one asked about my past. No one asked, "Are you okay?" or "What is your story?" It would be hard for me to answer that question anyway, but for a long time no one even asked.

When I lived with Natalie, she asked, and that's why I finally opened my heart and my mind. That's also why I struggled to live with her. I didn't trust anyone. If I let someone in, I knew I'd probably lose that person. I didn't care how bad it hurt Natalie to shut her out, but I didn't know I was hurting me, too. I was scared she would leave me; I was scared of losing her like I had everyone else, but every day God showed me little by little how He used Natalie in my life.

She was the person who took care of me then and stands by me now. She loved me every day, even when I wasn't lovable. She taught me what family should look like and accepted me for who I was, without judging. She protected me the best she could and provided everything I needed.

I was starting, finally, to understand my story.

47

When I went home for my brother's wedding in the spring of 2013, it was a refreshing time with family. I desperately needed encouragement because I was learning the language and, therefore, not yet doing what I had moved to the Philippines to do.

Daniel and I hadn't talked much, but of course, I knew he would want to talk to me while I was home. We met at a deli for lunch. I was hurt and angry at his actions. He had said he wanted our relationship and then threw it away.

I let him talk first, and he said how sorry he was and that what he did was wrong and unfair.

Ya think? Yeah, it was unfair. You led me on, knowing I was moving to Asia for Jesus!

That's not exactly how the conversation went, but I did get a chance to tell him how much he hurt me.

He was sincere and asked that we try again. He promised he would do better. I believe in second chances, so I agreed but told him it would be completely unacceptable for him to quit communicating with me again. "If you cannot do it, then just be honest and tell me instead of silence."

Everything was fine for several months, though it was hard building a relationship with someone far away and in different time zones. My home in the Philippines was thirteen hours ahead of Daniel's home in Mississippi. We both knew we had a connection; we had felt it our entire lives and prayed each step of the way.

I remember August 8, 2013, vividly—the last day he communicated with me, *again*. Thankfully, I was visiting my family on vacation in Hawaii after a few months in the Philippines since my brother's wedding. They had suggested they meet me "halfway," and even though they travelled a third of the way, the trip was a great idea, for it helped distract me from my pain.

After the Hawaii trip, my mom flew with me to the Philippines to help me move to CDO, the city where we started the ministry for street kids. I was so thankful to have her with me during that time.

When we arrived in the Philippines, Mom and I attended a conference for international adoption in Manila. Several adoption agencies shared their successes of the year and their goals moving forward. One agency spoke on the importance of bonding with the family after an adoption. They offered camps that helped children adapt to their new family and new home.

During the open forum, I asked the agent, "Have you ever thought about putting on a camp like this at an orphanage before the children get adopted? That way you can help prepare kids for a family but also help those who may never have that opportunity."

The adoption agent and forum speaker was speechless. After a long pause, he admitted he had never thought of that. Several people told me afterward they would be interested in having a camp like this at their orphanages once it was developed.

I learned so much at this conference, but because the ministry I was involved with helped street kids instead of orphans, I wondered how I could take these ideas and shape them for neglected children. God was developing a desire within me that He would eventually equip me for in order to make it a reality.

After the conference, months went by, and I often thought about what God had revealed to me but knew it was something for another time while I focused on launching the ministry.

The conference distracted me from Daniel for a few days, but then I'd hurt again. I was confused why the Lord would allow this relationship to start in the first place. I continued to pray for my future husband, not knowing what exactly happened for Daniel to stop communicating. Then one day, I received a message on Facebook from a woman who knew Daniel very well. She asked if I had heard from him or knew what was going on. She then shared bits and pieces of what was happening in his life.

Daniel loved his church, but it became difficult for him to thrive there. Eventually, misunderstandings caused them to let him go. He was young, and for a church he loved to let him go it was detrimental. He was dismissed on August 8, 2013, the same day he stopped communicating with me. His world and his dreams were crushed, and he couldn't see through it. He was devastated and belittled himself, and he thought I wouldn't understand or want him after that.

He definitely should have told me about this, but sometimes our initial reactions cause us to respond in ways we normally would not. Daniel entered into a dark season of his life where he questioned everything. It wasn't my place to step in, so I prayed for him and trusted that the Lord was still in control.

In the midst of that season, I started the ministry and built relationships with the kids. I learned how to introduce them to Jesus and help them survive. That was my focus during that time, and I tried to forget about the relationship Daniel and I almost had.

48

Many years ago, Natalie asked me what I wanted to do after finishing school. Most people would have said they wanted to get a good job, buy a house, and have a family. However, for some reason, that's not what I wanted. The first thing I said was that I wanted to help children who were like me. After that, I would help my family. I had no idea how to do that, but I had a feeling that one day I would have the opportunity to do that kind of ministry.

When you are a kid, you have many random ideas that pop in your head, but ever since I've lived at the orphanage, I've always had a desire to help others.

When I was fourteen years old, there were four siblings, two boys and two girls, who stayed in our orphanage for six months. The orphanage said they were there temporarily. The three-year-old would not obey our houseparents. She always cried, and when I tried to comfort her, she just held my hand and stared at me. She let me carry her every now and then, and I helped bathe and feed her. I played with her, and sometimes she slept beside me like a sister. Many days after school, I brought something home for her. I had to hide her in my room to give her the treat so the other kids wouldn't be jealous. I always wondered, *"Where is her family?"*

I found out her mom had passed away and her dad was irresponsible. The older brother, who was only seven, had taken care of them before they arrived at the orphanage. Most of the time they stole food to survive.

I saw my family through their family. That's how we were after my parents died. One day, when I returned from school, the children were gone. As usual, I had brought her something. My houseparent said their father had taken the children.

I was shocked... *Why?*

The housemother couldn't answer my question. I went straight to my room and cried. I didn't eat dinner that night; I just went to bed. I loved her like a little sister and didn't get to say goodbye to her. That's my why... That's why I decided to help kids like me when I grow up. God used her to change my life and give me a purpose.

One of my co-orphans came from the same town as her family and gave me updates every now and then. The last I heard, their father was getting worse and the kids were still alone and taking care of themselves. Their father made the two boys rob a house and give him the money. *"How can a father do that to his children?"* I could not imagine. I was so worried he might make my "little sister" do that one day, too. It became a dream of mine to somehow find her and help her, too.

49

At Uncle Dick's Home in December of 2010, I looked around the dark, bare room and tried my best to hold back the tears and the huge lump in my throat. My first three months in the Philippines were ending. Many of the kids joked with me on the way to breakfast, "You're gonna cry!"

I wasn't sure if this was the last time I would hear the beautiful children's voices lifting up their version of an old hymn. They sang in broken English:

"The steadfast love of the Lord never ceases. His mercies never 'are come' to an end. They are new every morning, new every morning. Great is Thy faithfulness, Oh Lord, great is Thy faithfulness!"

This old hymn is called "The Steadfast Love of the Lord," and it's found in many church hymnals. His faithfulness is great, and what a sweet reminder to hear that each morning from those precious mouths as they thanked the Lord for a new day and the meal set before them.

God has so much planned for each one of them and so many more around the globe. They are cared for; they are loved and one day may be adopted if they're lucky. The system takes years and years, and many kids end up passing the age restriction before their paperwork is matched with a family. It breaks my heart that, regardless of adoption, they still may not know who they are and what they can be if they don't learn to dream.

Many children like them have no idea how difficult their future will be if they never address the issues in their past. They don't know they need to think about that to avoid problems in the future. They need the space to open up.

Just as many of our parents and teachers prepared us for college and then life in the real world, orphaned and neglected children need to be prepared for their lives after the orphanage or after the streets. They cannot possibly understand their thoughts without someone helping them. In addition, the key is to address what they have been through while they are young, before they become ingrained with negative thoughts and lies about themselves and their worth.

One of my dreams is to help the children of the world know Jesus and allow Him to show them the desires of their heart and let them dream. A dream coupled with the hope of Christ can light a fire within them, to never give up until their dreams become reality.

50

While living in Malaybalay, I had a few of my neighbors' children over for games and lunch on Saturdays. One Saturday, the Malaybalay branch of K.I.M. had their Bible school program kickoff for the year. Kids from all over Malaybalay attended and heard the Gospel.

Brindy and I took our neighbors' kids to the kickoff. Each week, volunteers were needed in different areas. This particular week, I met Angelo, who was walking on a table at the back of the room. I watched his sister tend to him before she joined the group of kids for game time. I went over to see him because I thought he was excessively small to be left alone to walk on a table for three hours.

Immediately, he came to me and wanted to be in my arms, which was rare for Filipino babies. Usually, the color of my skin confused them, but this little angel didn't care. He wanted someone to love him. I noticed right away he hadn't been taken care of and had had a few accidents without wearing a diaper. He didn't have any clothes to change into, but Brindy and I found some and told his sister we were taking him to change and clean him up. When I did, I asked her how old he was... My guess was a year, or a year and a few months...

He was three! I could not believe it. He was tiny.

Brindy and I gave him a bath. He was the sweetest child but didn't talk. His swollen abdomen, a sign of malnutrition, explained his size and lack of communication. After we dressed him in clean clothes, we got him something to eat. He was obviously starved. After he ate, I held him and rocked him to sleep.

He woke up quite suddenly, and my lap was wet. Diapers are a luxury, which explains why he was so dirty before. When it was almost time for the group to be served their meal before going home, I wasn't sure if he'd be able to eat again. Brindy held him while I fed him, and he ate every bite of the warm, sticky rice bowl. When he finished, he wanted to get down, and he immediately raced outside. We chased him and quickly found out he needed to urinate, which he did—off the sidewalk. I was thankful he didn't soil my lap again. He was partly potty-trained after all!

51

It was time to move. After many long months in Malaybalay, the day came—a day I had longed and prayed for. Finally, my last day in Malaybalay, where I had spent my first eight months in the Philippines, where I learned a language and a culture, where I cried tears of joy and sadness. The place where I felt at home, yet felt like a stranger; where I felt alone, yet felt I belonged.

That place—that house—was where I learned more about life, Jesus, and myself than any other place in my life. Many times, I didn't leave that house and felt trapped by language study, but that trap opened so many doors of ministry, which made the house a jewel to me. It was where I wanted to give up and go home until I realized I *was* home. It was exactly where God wanted me to be, and that's where I consider home— with Him.

As I looked around my home for the last time that night, memories flooded my mind and overwhelmed me... *Could this really be happening? Do these boxes mean I made it?* I never thought the day would come when I'd move to CDO and begin the work I had come here to do. This was not just something I had accomplished or had endured through hard times... This was a milestone—one I will always cherish.

Malaybalay was home to many memories. Brindy and I chased an enormous flying roach on the first night in our house, which ended with me sliding baseball-style through our kitchen on the bug spray! The bug won that battle. We also had many unwanted rodent visitors we buried in the backyard. I won't forget the giant spiders Brindy took down with a spoon while I threatened to go to a hotel.

This was the place where I introduced Brindy to the TV show *Cake Boss*, and we almost finished watching every season. We bonded over that show and had to limit our episodes per night or we would never have slept. I then had the bright idea to make her very own cake from "Cake Boss Natalie" for her birthday. Let's just say I would never be hired if I were to apply as a baker. Technically the cake was three layers, but it looked like a big mess!

Brindy and I grew closer in that house. When Thata, the cook from the local orphanage and our friend, came to live with us, Brindy opened up even more. Having all three of us there allowed her to feel more at home because she wasn't the only Filipino.

If you look at Brindy today, you will see a very different person from the one I met at the orphanage. I don't believe this change would have happened had she gone from the orphanage to living with her family. Yes, I challenged her, but I also loved her and believed in her. That is what brought her to a different frame of mind about herself and a different level of maturity. She was no longer living to survive and suppressing her past; she was finally facing her past, and because of that, she was finally thriving.

In our Malaybalay home, Brindy and I bought a German Shepherd puppy. Together, we taught Samson to sit, stay, and obey the word "no." We laughed when the dog cried in fear at the top of our two stairs because we knew he would one day tower over them. He slept under the couch that was three times his size.

And that house was where he tried to hunt chickens in the yard.

That house became home to so many flourishing relationships.

We were able to bless and love Ate Bless and her son Angelo. God allowed me to hire her to help around the house, which is very common in the Philippines. Sure, I gave her a job, but she taught me more about giving and supporting than I could imagine. Over the years, God has enriched our relationship and allowed us to be there for one another.

That home was where my tutor Jonah's patience was always tested by my language frustrations, but she never gave up. Our relationship grew in that house while we encouraged each other and grew closer. I owe her for hanging in there with me.

Our neighbors Lexxie and Hilsam enjoyed my first homemade lasagna in the Philippines for "Neighbor Night." As we got to know them, our relationship grew. Lexxie asked me to be a bridesmaid in their wedding and later a Godmother to their precious baby girl, Gabby.

It was my first house, Brindy's first room, and the place where we learned to live together and bond through our different backgrounds.

Many mornings, we fought on the way to church. She hardly ever wanted to go, and I didn't understand why... She always went to church while at the orphanage. I wanted her to experience a bigger church with people who would be a part of her life and give her additional opportunities to serve others as well.

After a while, I learned she was angry at God and didn't want to love Him because she didn't feel loved. There was no amount of love I could show her to help her realize she needed to allow herself to feel the Lord's love. He was there!

We've all had things happen to us that cause us to question the Lord, but most of the time when we stick it out, we realize He uses it for good. He didn't always cause those things to happen. He allowed them but never left us alone.

That's why we're here; we're all here to be there for one another through life's difficulties. Whether you believe in Jesus or not, you support family and friends during tough times. That's what orphans and neglected kids around the world miss every day, and they feel so alone in their situations.

How can we fix their feelings of loneliness and inadequacy? How can we help them? We have to do something for the "Brindys" of the world. Walking through this with Brindy helped me realize there is something we can do about it.

That house was full of healing, conflict, pain, endurance, resolutions, growth, joy, laughter, and hope. Brindy and I became family there, and though we were excited for what was to come, we will forever cherish our days there—the good, the bad, the happy, and the sad.

52

It is hard to change lives. Letting go of the past starts in the heart and mind.

When the kids are ungrateful and disrespect us, I am reminded of myself at the orphanage. At those times, I am more understanding than ever. Now I know how much I hurt my houseparents, but I also know kids don't really mean the things they say. Deep inside, they are hurting. They need someone to help them break free from the suffering inside them.

One of our first kids, Jay Larry, lived at our center for a while. He was so respectful to me. If I had extra allowance, I bought clothes for him or took him to lunch. I felt as if he were my younger brother. However, I noticed he disobeyed the staff at the center. He had been through a lot, even thrown in jail once.

One day, he said he didn't want to stay in the center anymore. My heart ached because I felt as if I'd failed. I was losing a life that I knew mattered. I had showed him so much love, and he wasted it. I wanted so badly to keep him from danger. I wished I could have forced him to stay at the center because that's what was best for him. That's why we have to change the way these kids think and help them realize they want to change and to believe in the possibility of a brighter future off the street.

Jay went back to the street, and when I saw him later, he was dirty again and acting differently. I always prayed he would come back to the center and continue his education. I visited him and kept praying and believing he would come around. I didn't stop. I couldn't. It's in my blood. This is what I live for and what my life is about. It's more important to me than anything else. Even though it's difficult and some kids don't change, I will do my best to give every kid I can the opportunity to know Jesus and choose to follow Him.

Family, for me, is the basic unit of society. I decided to help our ministry because, in reality, we are all family and every kid should know they have a family in Christ.

53

"I'm gonna marry that girl one day!" Daniel always said when he saw my family's Christmas cards on Mrs. Joy's refrigerator. Mrs. Joy was a Sunday school teacher and a local Christian leader both Daniel and I respected.

Apparently, many people knew about his plan, but not many knew he met the criteria for my dream guy. I remember a time when I shared my desires for a future husband with Mrs. Joy at youth camp.

"I really feel like I want to marry a worship leader someday," I told her.

She always prayed with me and for me. I called her my prayer warrior. Many times, I wondered what it was like for her to hear about my desires and pray for me, along with hearing Daniel making claims over me. She never interceded in any way aside from prayer, which must have been difficult yet entertaining at the same time.

After my three months in the Philippines, my parents threw a surprise welcome home party for me. Many of my friends and family came to see me, hug me, encourage me, and hear what I had experienced and how it changed my life.

There was one guest, in particular, who showed up near the end because he had driven six hours after football practice to surprise me. Daniel even had to drive back to college in Arkansas the next morning. At the time, I didn't let him know the gesture was noticed.

Daniel and I hung out when we could, but always as "just friends." One night in January of 2011, we heard there was going to be a red moon, a special type of eclipse. However, it was to happen in the middle of the night. We were such daredevils, meeting up in the middle of the night to see the moon! Wouldn't you know, the sky was covered by clouds. *You have to be kidding me!* He came over anyway, and we sat on a bench near the pool and looked at the sky, hoping the clouds would dissipate. We just talked.

"Are you gonna kiss me or not?" The lyrics of a country song ran through my head.

This moment had built up for years, and we were finally alone. It was the perfect chance for him to make a move and let me know he liked me more than a friend.

As our conversation—and intermittent awkward silences—continued, he got close and then backed away, which continued for a while. Then, suddenly, he finally did it! *Whew! First kiss was in the books!* I wish I could say the rest was history and we lived happily ever after, but things were much more complicated than that.

Not long after, I moved back to Texas for seminary, but the walls were definitely broken down back then. It was obvious the age difference didn't matter to me anymore. There was something there and we felt it grow for years to come.

54

Brindy and I moved to Cagayan De Oro in August of 2013. CDO, home to approximately 600,000, was a large city, conveniently located on a small strip of land sandwiched between the ocean and the mountains— the best of both worlds. There were four major malls, at least two large outdoor markets, and not just one movie theater, but four.

The first day after settling in our new home, we went to the center of the city to a park called Divisoria (not to be confused with the Divisoria in Manila), and sat on a bench to pray for the area before launching our ministry. While I prayed quietly, three street kids approached me.

"Give me money," they said in broken English.

I quickly responded to them: "Unsa imong ngalan?" ("What's your name?")

They were shocked to say the least.

In their language, I continued to ask their ages, where they lived, and where their families were. Before long, the kids forgot what they had originally wanted from me, and we enjoyed a conversation getting to know one another.

A mission team was to visit the following day, so I invited the kids to meet us again for lunch and basketball. The next day, we waited for a while because we suspected they didn't know the time; but they never showed up.

When we were about to leave, a young boy approached us. His clothes were stained and torn, and you could practically see his bones through his skin. He had the best crooked, little smile.

JJ introduced himself by asking for money, a common trend we were noticing. He was collecting trash to recycle to help his family. We asked if he knew the boys we had met the previous day. He grinned from ear to ear and nodded. Then, he grabbed my hand and pulled me to follow him. We must have walked half a mile during the hottest time of the day. We stopped at a coconut stand, and JJ pointed as if we were supposed to know what he meant.

The owner of the stand said the boys we met worked for him on occasion but were not there that day. We told JJ that if he saw the boys to tell them we would be back the following day. He had a better chance of running into them than we did.

The next day, we returned and parked along the square. Immediately, I spotted one of the boys, and he ran over to us and said hello. We were dressed and ready to play basketball, and when we invited him, his excitement resembled that of a child in a toy store.

He disappeared to gather his friends, the start of a relationship that would open many doors for their lives. Through basketball, meals, and hanging out, we got to know the kids who called the streets of CDO their home.

55

"Fight the good fight for the true faith. Hold tightly to the eternal life to which God has called you, which you have confessed so well before many witnesses" (1 Timothy 6:12).

Fight the fight—that's exactly what it was... It's a battle against evil that comes to steal, kill, and destroy, but God has already won! Though He conquered the grave, we still struggle to choose Him and follow Him. Why is it so hard to choose Him every day?

Each day, we fought against something but with victory on our side. We had hope and endurance that couldn't be found without the victory of Jesus. I struggled to understand why the kids in our ministry had a hard time choosing between school and a safe future or addictions and starvation.

I would remember: they're just kids. They shouldn't have to make those decisions. They like the freedom of the streets. Didn't we all want freedom when we were younger?

One night, I saw the light shining through the addictions and "freedom" of the street, pointing toward the future and the life I continually hoped to help these kids find.

In October of 2013, thirteen men arrived in the Philippines on their fourth month of The World Race. The World Race is a mission trip to eleven countries in eleven months. The first day they arrived, we took them to our ministry center and shared our goals for the month they were visiting. During orientation alone, we reached a milestone. While I was explaining our goal to get the kids voluntarily coming to our center and interested in our ministry, four of our kids showed up—out of the blue! We stopped our meeting and began playing. Until that day, the kids had only come to the center when we guided them.

The first week, we visited existing ministries in the community, played basketball, unloaded a twenty-foot container of donations, and built relationships with our kids in Divisoria, the plaza in the middle of town where many street kids hung out and many called home.

The second week, those relationships developed when we started an official night ministry where the kids were easy to find because they hung out in Divisoria all night. It was important to maintain a presence in their element to be a part of their lives outside our walls. It seemed to be working quite well and the community also noticed. We wanted our impact and our love of Christ to be seen beyond the kids in Streetlight. That light needed to transform the entire community to break the barrier between street kids and everyone else. Many nights, locals approached us and asked, "Why are you playing with those kids? What are you doing here?"

On the mission team's fourth and final week, five of our kids went to youth camp at Cagayan De Oro Bible Church with five of the guys. We weren't sure if the kids would even be interested in going, but to our surprise and God's goodness, even Nelson wanted to go to camp.

Nelson was fifteen, the leader of the pact, and sometimes he thought our activities were not cool enough for him. The kids enjoyed it so much they asked to go to church with us the next Sunday.

The last night the World Race team was there was another breakthrough moment. I hadn't noticed the light in the kids' eyes before. They were like kids playing with a group of "big brothers," a sight I had dreamed of, prayed for, longed for, and finally witnessed. What I saw was not just a vision, it was hope. And hope has a destination. I had never seen those boys and girls smile, laugh, and play the way they did that night. My vision grew, because no longer did I just hope for smiles and laughter.

My vision is now much bigger and has expanded to more neglected kids and their lives beyond the street. Those guys made an impact that lasted longer than their time in the Philippines. The kids never forget those who invest in them, and I will never forget that night and similar milestones that awaken the light within them.

While we made progress, the time came to implement practical ways that would enable them to change their probable future and reinforce the same hope many of us had growing up. It was time they started dreaming and answering the question we all once answered: *What do you want to be when you grow up?*

56

One day, I sat and thought about why I hated myself...
Why do I hate my family? Why do I hate God? Why do I
feel alone and that I am not good enough to stay with
Natalie? That night, I realized I had been listening to
lies Satan was telling me. I let him guide me for many
months, but I decided it was over.

I realized God was always there for me; He never
left. He has taken care of me since I lost my parents. He
placed people around to care for me and even take me
to the orphanage. He was in control of that, too. Even
more, He sent people to the orphanage who would
invest in my future. I didn't realize that at the time,
because I was so full of hatred toward Him and the
people around me.

I was wrong. I was tired of thinking about it. I
wanted to let it go, but it was so hard. Sometimes, those
feelings returned when I felt alone. I have learned to
face life with love, and I found courage from those
surrounding me in hope every day. They made me feel I
mattered in this world and that I had an assignment to
finish, which was helping neglected orphans or
children in our society.

This is my life, and I'm finally taking back control to
experience the peace and happiness I wanted all along.
I hope to be able to use what I've learned from the
bondage of my past to help my siblings, my future

family, and others who experience the same thing. Finally, I am becoming who I was made to be!

57

After moving to the Philippines, I prayed God would send others—helpers and friends. There were days when I felt so alone and misunderstood that I would cry myself to sleep. I never lost my peace in knowing I was where I was supposed to be, but I lost my strength more times than I can count. I know we're not guaranteed to have things easy when we follow the Lord, but I longed for helpers. Looking back, I realize that time was special while God shaped me to come to the Lord alone and share everything with Him.

Once Brindy and I moved to Malaybalay, we met some newly-arrived Americans. There weren't many, so we eventually came to know one another. Meagan and Leah, two American girls from Alabama and Texas, had been on The World Race, connecting with different ministries. During their "race," they stayed in Malaybalay for a month in November of 2012.

When they got home, they prayed about what God was calling them to do next. They talked one day and were surprised God had put the same thing on their individual hearts—to return to the Philippines and help street kids.

When we met and realized we were all trying to do the same thing, they jumped on board with the ministry and began learning the language. We started with simple outreach to street kids, but we saw much more than what was on the surface.

The overarching focus of our ministry is one much more than simply street kids or orphans, but neglected children in general. Orphanages exist as a home for children with no parents. In some cases, children have one or both parents living, but they are not taken care of at home for various reasons. Most orphanages do not cater to housing street kids because becoming a street kid is usually a slow process of neglect or rebellion. By that point, a street kid may have been influenced by the street to the extent that he or she may not be suitable to mix with children who haven't been exposed to situations such as drugs or alcohol.

However, I've realized a common theme exists among orphans and street kids: they have both been neglected or abandoned in some way at some point. They have experienced trauma that cannot be ignored. When a child, or anyone for that matter, experiences such distress, it is imperative to seek resolve in that conflict. He or she may never be able to move on with his or her life if these fundamental issues are not resolved.

In orphanages, everyone has similar problems or experiences, and many times kids are encouraged to try to live as though the problems they've experienced never happened. But their lives aren't normal, so why pretend that they are?

In the end, ignoring issues becomes detrimental to the children. In some instances, children may be instructed not to talk about their situation for privacy or investigative reasons. While I respect that, it doesn't mean the child must pretend as if nothing ever happened. The child requires healing—emotionally, physically, spiritually, and mentally. That cannot happen while pretending their issues don't exist. In cases where information about a child's trauma must be kept legally confidential, someone such as a social worker, counselor, or houseparent should intentionally invest in the healing of the child. Several exercises exist to help children cope without releasing information to peers or the public outside of the orphanage or ministry's administration. Children need to face their trauma head-on as early as possible or they will have a much harder road ahead.

Brindy went through a season where she hated her life so much that she truly wanted to die. Many nights I stayed awake to ensure she didn't attempt anything detrimental. At times, I heard her throwing things against the wall—coins, bottles—and shortly thereafter heard her sweeping glass. I lay in my bed and prayed. That's all I could do.

One night, she came to my room and said she was leaving because she didn't want to be a burden anymore. She felt it would make my life better if she were gone. I explained my life would be better if I saw her succeed and if she allowed people to love and care for her, especially Jesus. The season of begging Brindy to give herself a chance lasted at least a year and came in waves while she continually fought against a lack of self-worth and a desire to run away. I believe she was trying to run from what was within her, yet she was confusing it with wanting to run from me. This was a cycle of self-punishment as she pushed away the people who loved her the most.

On our trip to the U.S. in 2014, she stopped eating or threw up anything she ate. We took her for an endoscopy and found that because of her self-inflicted malnutrition, she had obtained a bacterial infection. On that same trip, we saw a counselor because the situation was more than I could handle. Though the counselor never truly "diagnosed" her, he did explain she experienced emotions of depression resulting from not having dealt with her past.

Rob was a Christian counselor who had experience in overseas missions, so I was eager for his advice. Brindy was angry with me at first because I didn't tell her about the appointment, but I knew she wouldn't go if I had. She needed help, and I couldn't handle the situation anymore.

Rob took her through a series of questions and exercises that brought so much out of her. He helped her interpret her feelings and explained how she misinterpreted things because she held a skewed view of relationships warped by her past. She realized she stopped growing up when she arrived at the orphanage because she was among others like herself. She had suppressed all she had been through, and when she left the orphanage, she had to face everything for the first time. She almost lost herself in the process.

Parenting biological children from birth is hard enough, I've heard, but parenting an orphaned teenager has additional challenges. The parent or guardian must determine how the orphan copes and reacts to leadership and discipline. This was particularly difficult at my age without a husband, experience, and with cultural differences.

However, this is what I am passionate about, and I hope to encourage change, helping children around the world understand themselves. Brindy's experience can take place in most neglected children's lives one day, which could be foundational to their futures. Through Brindy, God gave me a glimpse into what these children need. My determination will not let me rest without attempting to teach neglected children around the world to dream, find hope, and ultimately become who they were created to be.

58

The ups and downs in this type of ministry are, in many ways, inexplicable.

Brindy isn't the only orphan in need. There are so many kids out there with similar stories, traumatized in one way or another and growing up without having the opportunity to deal with it. The situations these stories convey cause kids to stay in the cycle in which they were born or the mindset in which they were left—unless someone steps in to help.

One of our girls at Streetlight was caught, simply from being out past the city curfew for minors, and taken to a hospital. There was nowhere to take girls in CDO when they were "rescued" from the street, so they were taken to the city hospital's psyche ward. That was problem number one: a psyche ward.

Problem number two: the authorities of the psyche ward shaved the children's heads to shame them and keep them from escaping. This girl in particular did escape from the psyche ward but not soon enough. We found her devastated and shamed, covering her head with a scarf. We were broken-hearted with her. This once-confident, bold, and independent young girl was weakened by a cruel and intolerable punishment for breaking curfew. This type of punishment only made the walls around her heart thicker as she shielded herself with anger and masked her feelings with drugs.

Many would agree this punishment for breaking curfew was much too harsh and resulted in more harm than good. Our ministry took a different approach by giving children a place to go other than the street, but it was imperative, first and foremost, to build a relationship and allow them to feel safe.

On another occasion, a taxi hit one of our boys, Meo. We received the call late one Sunday night and went to check on him. We tried to find out what happened. The kids had been chasing one another in the street, which was typical, but this time there was a consequence. His ankle was scraped pretty badly, so we cleaned it, gave him medicine to fight the onset of infection, and wrapped his ankle. We assumed that was the extent of the injuries because no one could explain what had happened after he was hit.

He hopped around for about two weeks. At that point, we worried because he still couldn't put pressure on his foot. After the swelling had gone down, one night I noticed it looked crooked. The next morning, we took him for an X-ray, and sure enough, the bone was broken—in half. The doctor said it would heal correctly because it was still broken and that the wound needed to heal first before putting on a cast.

We allowed Meo to be the first kid to stay in our center overnight. Since his accident, he needed extra care and protection in order to heal correctly. Our number one rule before allowing kids to stay in the center was that they had to stop sniffing Vulcaseal or Rugby, the glue of choice that masked their worries. Meo had rarely been involved with that scene anyway, so he happily agreed. While he lived at the drop-in center, we saw a change in his life off the street.

That was when we knew the model we had been given to build our ministry and the vision God had given us at the time was the right path. Allowing Meo to stay at the center kept him away from the effects of the street, including drugs, negative freedom, and lack of education. He made better grades in our education program and even asked for extra assignments between classes. He was eager to help around the center and attended mid-week Bible studies at the church with our houseparents. He even gained a little weight since he was able to eat three regular meals and he started to look his age. His progress gave us hope for the rest of the kids in our ministry.

Another issue we faced was abusive parenting. For example, we had a girl named Ami, who wouldn't go home because she wanted to get high on drugs. Her sister Dell didn't use drugs and went home every night. However, when Dell arrived home, her father yelled and hit her because she didn't bring her little sister Ami home with her. This pattern didn't seem to be changing. Instead of showing pride in his daughter, who had made a better decision, the father found a reason to beat her. We housed the girls for a week and a half while we sorted through their problems.

Since then, their mother took more control in protecting them. Dell lived at our drop-in center on and off for about a year. Helping make changes in these kids' lives is a process and can often involve discussions with the whole family, and this is an example of how differently each kid responds to the help they need.

We were able to maintain good relationships with the parents of the kids in our ministry. They were appreciative of the services we offered their children. Each family signed an agreement that their children could participate in our programs and services. Many of the families attended our holiday parties and livelihood trainings and programs.

We started a jewelry-making program for the mothers, giving them a chance for an income away from the street. Many collected trash for recycling or helped park cars. We had always desired to give them an alternative because our ultimate goal was to reunite families and give them the tools necessary to succeed and care for their children again.

We have learned a lot about street kids' families, as well as how kids behave when we take care of them. One of the deepest issues we discovered through these situations is that our kids needed to relearn how to be kids. A child should not have to choose between sleeping on the street or returning home, nor whether to listen to his or her parents. Yet, somewhere along the way, they were given a freedom, either through a situation of neglect, abuse, rebellion, or abandonment that changed their reasoning and skewed their understanding of how to be cared for and loved. They have been so estranged from the discipline a parent should offer that they have forgotten how to be obedient and trust what is for their good.

59

Once Brindy and I began helping street kids, she noticed a need to further her education. Because she had so much personal experience, I encouraged her to think of a degree that would allow her to make a career out of her passion and desire to help other kids similar to her.

She felt created to become someone to help kids work through their issues. As we tried to figure out ways to help the kids in our ministry, I realized Brindy was unofficially acting as a social worker in the way she handled situations based on her personal experience.

She also felt a social work degree would equip her with the information needed to better what she was already doing. She was anxious yet motivated to have the opportunity to further her education and make a deeper, more educated impact on many kids' lives.

On our trip to the US in 2014, after hearing her story, a family friend decided to support Brindy in her education. She began classes soon after.

60

We started our own organization helping street kids. It wasn't an orphanage, but street kids and orphans are just like me and face the same things I faced. Most of them have a mother and/or father, but they abandoned or neglected them. We are the same in that we both need a family's love and support. I see myself in them. Many times, they act with the same stubborn attitude I used to have. Deep inside they want to change. They want to be accepted and understood, but society rejects them and doesn't give them a chance. Most of the kids don't know they can have a different future. They don't even think about the future. They live day by day.

Once we share the love of Christ with them, they begin to have hope. Once they feel loved, they find their purpose because they understand they matter. My desire is the kids in our ministry will believe us when we say they can be whatever they want to be. Look at me; I am the perfect example.

Natalie found me, and God brought us together so we could help kids like me through Ellipsis International. We are different from other organizations because we give them the opportunity to break free from the lies in their mind. We also want to make sure all the kids have the chance to work through their emotions. We want them to know Jesus and themselves. They've experienced trauma in one way or another, and if they don't handle it as soon as possible, it will traumatize them later in life as it did me.

I have difficulties, but have learned what is true and what is right. I hope the same happens for them. They can learn it is our past that makes us stronger. We chose our slogan for Ellipsis, helping kids meet the Author of their story, because there is freedom in following Jesus and allowing Him to use our past to give us strength for our future.

I learned so much at the orphanage that I use now in our ministry. I am able to help teach kids right from wrong and give them advice since I remember what I went through. Many teenagers go home in the middle of the night. They stay out drinking and disrespect their parents. I am still young, but I don't desire to do the things my friends are doing. I grew up in a different environment with many rules. Even though I can do anything I want now, I don't. I would rather stay in my room than roam around. Often, I choose to hang out with kids in our ministry rather than with my friends.

The orphanage taught me to value things that matter in life—making memories and building strong relationships. Because I am able to work on what I am passionate about, I don't mind missing a social life. I see myself in the kids, and I want to be a good sister to them so they don't go through what I went through so late in life. I'm here for them to talk to and cry with.

God has already given me opportunities to share my experiences with them. Most of the time, they cannot believe my past. Because I lived with Natalie and have a college degree, they think I came from a strong, wealthy family. When they find out the truth, they are shocked, but it makes them listen closely to my advice because I've been in their shoes. I've walked where they walk, and I want them to see what is ahead before they arrive. I want them to know they don't have to walk alone. They are not forgotten to me because I wasn't forgotten.

61

We were just going to get lunch.

It was a holiday weekend, the 2015 Higalaay Festival in Cagayan De Oro. People had been planning events all year for this festival, and we were excited to have a long weekend and enjoy the activities.

We took the opportunity to sleep in that Friday morning on August 28 because we knew we'd be up late with the firework show. I took my dog, Samson, for a run, enjoying the new neighborhood we had lived in for seven short weeks. Though it was late morning, the tall, skinny trees lining the road made the heat bearable. This was pretty much the only place in the city where I could run without dodging traffic or being stared at, besides the predictable stares at my giant one-hundred-pound German Shepherd. We took our time, taking it all in on a day with no responsibilities.

When I got home, I showered and cleaned the house. I even started dinner in the crockpot. It was set to be a fun, restful day.

Daniel was a little anxious, waiting for me to finish putting everything in the crockpot. We were both hungry for lunch and it was almost 1:30 p.m. We had planned to try a new restaurant in town, and he was getting "hangry" (hungry and angry).

We were about to walk out the door when I remembered I wanted to add another can of tomatoes to the crockpot. One extra minute and one ingredient that we could have lived without.

"I'm hurrying. I'm hurrying! You'll be glad I did this tonight when we get home for dinner," I said.

When we walked out the door, I noticed Daniel had his backpack with his laptop. "Why are you bringing your laptop? We are just going to lunch. It's a holiday, not a workday."

"You never know, I may need it."

We hopped on the scooter and debated whether we should take the car for the day.

"Samson is almost out of food. It will be hard to bring his food home on the bike," I said.

"We'll figure it out. It is so much easier to get around and park if we take the bike. We can get the food later."

I remember each detail and decision of that morning: the things that took a minute longer than usual and the things we didn't do because it would have taken a few more minutes. That day, those decisions mattered down to the millisecond.

We strapped on our helmets and drove away. Surprisingly, there wasn't much traffic for a holiday. We cruised like normal, the wind blowing in our faces making it seem cooler than it was.

As we approached the gate of our subdivision on the four-lane highway, someone in the opposite inside lane stopped to turn left. We gave him the friendly beep, letting him know we were coming and to make sure he saw us. Normally, people turn right away if they don't see anyone coming. The SUV stopped, turned on his blinker, and waited. His stopping implied he'd seen us and was going to wait until we passed before turning, so we continued with caution.

In the Philippines, public transportation, cars, and SUV's drive as if they have the right of way at all times. Scooters are the underdogs and are treated that way.

Normally, a car would inch out anxiously, yet authoritatively, suggesting the bike should stop for him. The SUV wasn't inching out; the driver stopped, turned on the blinker, and waited—out of the ordinary. We usually wave in thanks at those people when we pass by.

As we neared and were about to pass, the driver of the SUV suddenly turned—not slowly, but with complete disregard.

Daniel beeped, louder and faster, trying to avoid him and even stop, but there wasn't enough time. If Daniel had slammed on the brakes, we would have fishtailed and possibly slid under the SUV or into other lanes of oncoming traffic. He did the best he could, trying to avoid an impending accident.

Of all the times we've had narrow escapes in traffic in Asia, this one was much different. Usually, I would yell or clutch Daniel if I thought we were about to be hit or hit something. This time, we both knew what was happening yet somehow remained calm; at least I did. I didn't yell or tense up, and I believe that helped save my life.

Right before the collision, Daniel glanced back and shouted, "I'm sorryyyyyy!" He doesn't remember that, but that's when I closed my eyes.

62

When Daniel found out Brindy and I were visiting the U.S., he reached out to me for the first time in several months. He said he wanted to explain things. I agreed to meet him because I needed clarity as well. However, I vowed I was moving on, and this was just a talk to help me do so. After all, we were on two different paths, and it was obvious there was no way this relationship would work out.

When we talked, he shared with me what had happened in the church and why he had not contacted me during that time. He apologized several times and clarified he was not asking me to try again. He then told me he was planning to join a mission team that would spend two years abroad. He had spent time in India and Thailand and felt a pull toward Southeast Asia. The organization asked him to turn in his list of the top three countries he wanted to be stationed in.

"I would like to put the Philippines as my top pick if you are okay with that? If that makes you uncomfortable, then I will leave it off my list," he said.

I was completely stunned, and my mind raced. *If he is potentially moving to the Philippines, maybe this could actually work. But is he doing this for me or himself?*

I battled, wanting closure yet also wanting to make sure I had given us the proper chance before giving up. *If he is seriously moving to Asia, we might as well try again.*

In April of 2014, Daniel agreed to visit the Philippines with the ministry I worked under to see if he was interested in joining us instead of another organization.

When he entered the picture, a fear erupted within Brindy that I was about to leave her as everyone else had left her. I had to teach her I wasn't like the others in her life. I wasn't going anywhere. We had become family, but even that word didn't make sense to her or make her feel at ease.

I used an example to help explain. I shared with her that when I went to college, I didn't live with my family, but we were still family.

"When my brother got married, he and his wife got their own house. Does that mean he is no longer our family?" I asked.

She began to understand the dynamics and commitment of a family and what that is supposed to mean. I also explained how things might change over time, but the family remains a unit. She had not had a traditional family experience since losing her parents. In an orphanage family, one is not exposed to the different stages a more typical family goes through. She struggled with this for the longest time, but she has come far.

When Daniel and I began dating, Brindy lost progress. She stopped communicating with us—not just the silent treatment—she literally wouldn't even look at us. Brindy felt like Daniel was replacing her and she didn't matter anymore. It took more than a conversation to work through this. We were entering a new season of life, and she didn't think she was ready.

At first, we tried to see if she would naturally work through it, but that wasn't happening. Daniel tried his hardest to show her he loved her, too, and wasn't trying to take me away. We made a tiny breakthrough when she laughed at a joke he made during dinner one night. I can't remember the joke, but I also won't forget that moment.

One day, Brindy disappeared because she was angry and felt left out when Daniel and I went on a date. I called her for what seemed like a million times trying to find her. There was nothing I could do but wait. She could have been anywhere.

When she got home, she was completely out of breath… We had a talk. She knew it was irresponsible for a young girl to go wandering in a large city at night. CDO was home to approximately 600,000 people. She told me she ran for her life because someone was following her. *My point exactly.*

She said she left the house to get food and was mad about having to move out soon. It was becoming obvious that Daniel and I were serious. She knew there would come a day when she would have to begin her own chapter, living on her own and learning to become independent. Brindy needed to learn some independence. She simply did not want to. When she reacted like this, she forced me to become harsh and to love her with "tough love" and discipline. Brindy became like my child though our age difference didn't allow that to feel natural. Her actions made it seem better that I treat her differently than I would a friend.

It was a process, but progress was made. The day she finally moved into her "boarding house," as they called it, she took a step that would be beneficial for her future outside of my relationship with Daniel.

After we moved the last item into her boarding room, I said I was proud of her and reassured her she would be fine. She came to the balcony to watch us drive away, and in that moment, I felt what I believe many parents feel when they drop their kids off at college. The feeling is difficult to explain, but it was a sense of pride for her bravery and a glimpse of hope through her step of faith. She would learn and grow if she allowed herself to, even though she didn't know that, in the end, the whole process was for her good. I prayed she would remember a verse we talked about often, "For we live by faith, not by sight" (2 Corinthians 5:7).

63

The actual impact happened in slow motion, and I'm thankful God created our bodies to go numb at that level of pain. The adrenaline took over.

Upon impact, the force threw me about ten or more feet in the air. My legs flew over my head when I flipped a few times and rolled to a stop. Thankfully, because I didn't tense up, the fall didn't cause too much damage besides severe bruising and overall soreness.

I immediately looked for Daniel. He shouted in a terrified voice when he saw me. "Natalie!"

After finding him alive, I noticed my leg was hurting. When I looked down, I couldn't believe what I saw. I shrieked in an eerie, glass-shattering tone about five times, a sound I'd never heard before come out of my mouth. Daniel tried to stand but couldn't. His entire kneecap was exposed. He crawled over to me, writhing in pain.

My entire shinbone was visible from the eight-inch long, two-inch deep gash running down my leg, resembling a sliced open watermelon. *Stop the bleeding!* I immediately grabbed my leg and applied pressure to hold my skin together.

Daniel lay beside me, trying to comfort me. I knew he was in immense pain and I had to do something.

My helmet dangled off the side of my head, still strapped on. I yelled at people staring at us, "Take my helmet off! Help!"

It was as if they were afraid to come near us.

Finally, with a little persistence, a woman unhooked my helmet and placed it behind my back for support. My purse was still strapped around me, so I asked her to take out my phone and call John, who was more like a Filipino father than our landlord and friend.

John lived a block away from the accident, and he could get us the help we needed. I tried my best to handle everything since I speak the local language, but I was exhausted and in pain.

It was extremely hot while we lay on the gravel road, waiting for assistance. A small woman ran toward me with an umbrella to shade me from the heat. She helped fix my dress as well because people were taking pictures and videos of us. That seemed to be the thing to do in the Philippines, though I have no idea why.

I asked her to hold my leg because my arms were shaking and tired. I assured her she wouldn't hurt me when I asked her to squeeze tighter. A man brought some bandanas to tie around my leg.

With my hands free, I struggled to make a phone call to my mom. I had just texted with her twenty minutes prior. I thought maybe she would still be awake on the other side of the planet. I couldn't remember how to dial internationally from my Filipino phone, but the third time I dialed, the phone rang.

"Mom, we were in an accident. We're okay. Our legs are hurt really bad. Please pray for us." I hung up, tears streaming down my face. That would have been the scariest voicemail she had ever received.

I texted others to ask them to pray and help if they were nearby.

It felt like no more than thirty seconds had passed before John arrived. He ran over and said, "You're going to be okay." His face was half-shaven, half-covered in shaving cream. He had dropped everything to come as quickly as he could.

I relaxed, in a way, knowing he would make sure we were taken care of. I wanted him to make sure we went to the best hospital possible because I knew we needed emergency surgery.

He told the emergency responders where to take us, and they loaded us into two different ambulances. I didn't like being separated, but they couldn't fit both of us into one. They strapped my leg onto a short wooden board stretching from my knee to my ankle.

When we drove off, the pain set in. The roads are far from smooth in the Philippines, and I felt every bump.

64

Daniel decided to move permanently to the Philippines in August 2014. He enjoyed working with our ministry and felt there was no significant reason for him to join the other organization over ours.

We went home to Mississippi for Christmas in December that year to be with family and update supporters on the ministry. We had several trips planned to speak at churches, but we also scheduled a mini vacation in the midst of everything. Daniel had never been to New York, so we went on a trip to the city for his birthday. My mom came to enjoy more time with us while we were in America and make sure Daniel enjoyed the best experience of New York City.

When we arrived, Daniel, Mom, and I went straight to Broadway. His first Broadway experience was an original, *Phantom of the Opera.* He was astonished he'd missed this for so long; music is his passion. We also took him shopping on Fifth Avenue and even visited *The Today Show* so he could see where I had interned.

Halfway through the trip, we visited the World Trade Center Memorial. We reflected on where we were that day and how it changed America and made us all stronger. After that, we visited the toy store FAO Schwartz to show Daniel the enormous piano. He was enjoying everything, but he wasn't as excited as I had thought he'd be, and said he was ready to go to Central Park—just the two of us.

Daniel had apparently googled the best entrance to the park, *so he said*... It was on the opposite side of the toy store, and we didn't have enough time to walk that far, so we attempted to get a taxi. It was a busy time of day, and he became frustrated when three taxis passed by with passengers.

I said, "Daniel, relax, we have plenty of time."

When we reached the entrance he had wanted, we followed his Google map to what was, apparently, a special spot. We dodged horse droppings on the road until he realized we were going the wrong way. I tried to make him feel like he was leading the way, since he had googled for information, even though I had been to Central Park several times and knew the area.

Finally, we got on the right path, took deep breaths, and just enjoyed walking together. A few minutes later, Daniel pointed to a random elderly woman. "How old do you think she is?"

What? Who cares? I thought, but replied, "I don't know, maybe sixty-five?"

He said, "No, I think she's eighty-five."

"She looks pretty good for an eighty-five-year-old out here walking around like that," I responded sarcastically.

We were heading toward a huge line of porta-potties, so Daniel suggested we cross the street. He pointed to a grassy hill, and suggested we check out the view of New York City from there.

"Why?" I asked.

"Let's just go. I think it will be cool."

While we gazed upon the skyline, he asked, "How many people do you think live in New York City?"

What is it with all these random questions?

I guessed a super low number, and he laughed and said, "I think it's a lot more than that, but out of all the people in this city and in the world, there's no one else I would rather spend my life with. Do you remember that woman I asked you about?"

Wide-eyed, I quietly replied, "Yes."

"Well, I want to be with you when I'm eighty-five."

"Well, I hope you live that long!" I responded before thinking. I had no idea what I meant by that, but it was an awkward time to be sarcastic. We both laughed.

He continued, "I love you with all of my heart, and I want to spend the rest of my life with you." He then got down on one knee and asked, "Will you marry me?"

"Yes!" I responded lightning-fast and immediately kissed him. A few people clapped when he stood.

Someone was creeping around us with a camera, and I turned to find Kate, one of my best friends from Texas, who is an amazing photographer. Standing beside her was my sister, who was not supposed to be in New York. I was overwhelmed and shockingly, speechless.

We then joined my mom, who was waiting at The Plaza Hotel with champagne and a few more of my best friends from Dallas and Boston. We shared the story of the eighty-five-year-old woman near the porta-potties and the lump with a view that ended in forever for Daniel and me. We had a million phone calls to make, starting with my dad, brother, and some of my best friends.

65

I had texted my sister and my brother to tell them we were in an accident. In the ambulance with sirens wailing, I called my dad. He answered.

"Dad," I said with a shaky voice. I tried to hold it together because I knew how helpless he would feel. "We were in an accident, but we're okay. Our legs are hurt really badly. Please pray. We want to be able to walk again."

I heard my mom in the background. "Joe, what is it?"

He said, "Okay, we will be praying."

I asked him to call Daniel's parents. "Just pray," I added. "We'll keep you updated. I love you."

"I love you, too," he said before he hung up.

The EMT leaned over and said, "Ma'am, we need to take you to Maria Reyna Hospital because they handle medical cases and trials."

I was so distraught and in pain with every bump we hit that I just agreed. John had made sure we were sent to the best hospital in town, CUMC, but apparently the woman made me agree to change that while we were en route. That turned out to be a bad decision, one I was in no shape to have made.

We arrived at the ER, and I was wheeled inside. Not long after, Daniel arrived. We were placed in the same room near the open-air entrance. The doors were wide open, so we saw nurses come and go, taking our vitals. An investigator bombarded me with questions, asking me to describe exactly how the wreck happened. In retrospect, I should have spoken in Visayan instead of English because she got the wrong information from what I told her. I didn't know it was an issue at the time and was in no shape to be interviewed or put my language skills to the test.

Leah and Meagan showed up, which made us much more at ease knowing someone could assist us to get help. We had to ask repeatedly where the doctor was and why we were waiting in pain with our wounds exposed to infection.

The nurses replied confidently, "We texted him."

"*You what?*" I replied emphatically, almost sitting up in shock. "Where is he? Please *call* him." I was so afraid the longer we waited the worse our recovery would be, not to mention our chances of walking again.

I was thankful to have Leah and Meagan there, updating our parents and putting pressure on the nurses to get the doctor as quickly as possible. We had to pay for X-rays, bandages, and pain medicine before they would do anything. To top it off, they wouldn't accept a credit card for the X-rays, so we had to borrow money from friends to keep from having to find an ATM.

"I promise you we're going to pay you. Just get the doctor here," I said.

Katrien and Stoffel, our friends from South Africa who were living in CDO, showed up to pray with us and help however they could.

Then John and Michelle arrived. We thanked John for helping us get to a hospital. He said he told them to take us to CUMC, and I explained what had happened.

"It's okay," he said. "The doctors travel between hospitals to see different patients. We will get you the best general surgeon in CDO."

I felt better, but hours went by before we saw the doctor. When he arrived, we recognized him from church and could not have been more relieved to know the hands that would determine the future of our legs belonged to a believer. Dr. Linog comforted us and left to prepare for surgery.

It was the longest, most stressful, and frightening day we had ever experienced. The accident happened at 1:30 p.m. in the afternoon, and we didn't go into surgery until 9 p.m.

They wheeled us both back to the operating room, and before they separated us, Dr. Linog grasped each of our free hands and prayed, "Lord Jesus, I ask that you would guide me in this surgery. Guide my hands and my eyes, and calm the nerves of Natalie and Daniel. Be with us in this surgery."

Tears streamed down my face, but I felt a slight sense of comfort. One by one, Daniel's fingers slipped out of my hand when they wheeled me into the next room to prep him for surgery. We asked they not give us full anesthesia but instead a block of the area for surgery, basically an epidural. I still feared we wouldn't make it through surgery or they would do something we didn't agree to, which was why I wanted to be awake.

Many times, I would feel that if I didn't fight for things in the Philippines, then no one would. You see, many people do not survive accidents in third world countries. In the Philippines, no one receives medical care until payment, which is the reason why many people die from even minor injuries. People are simply in accidents and it's their time to go; that's the outlook on many mishaps in the Philippines. If we had been unconscious, who knows what would have happened.

The scar I have on my leg doesn't compare to the trauma we experienced. If the gash had been one inch to the left, it would have hit an artery. Something as simple as losing too much blood in the hours we waited could have killed me or caused me to lose my leg.

In the room next to Daniel, a nurse asked, "Do you want me to leave the door open?"

I nodded. Though it was strange to be in the next room with the door open while someone was in surgery, I felt I could help in some way if they needed me.

66

While in New York, my mom surprised me with an appointment to pick out a wedding dress at Kleinfeld's, the place famous for the TV show *Say Yes to the Dress*. And that day, I did "say yes to the dress!" We found a place that could do alterations overnight since I wouldn't be able to go back and forth from the Philippines for fittings. While I was trying on my dress, I FaceTimed Brindy to share the news as I wanted to be sure she heard it straight from me. She screamed! She was so excited for us.

When Daniel and I returned from America, Brindy asked to move in with Meagan and Leah to save money and not to be alone. At this point, she had lived on her own for about six months. It was evident she had learned a good bit about independence and understood I wasn't leaving her by marrying. Because of her past, I explained she would be their roommate; they would not be her caregiver. She needed to help and do her part as a roommate. What she learned by living alone demonstrated to me that I had made the right decision—that time was good for her. If she hadn't had that time to grow, she wouldn't have learned how to take responsibility for herself.

That same night, I asked her to be my bridesmaid and said I had a dress for her. She was ecstatic but extremely nervous. I couldn't imagine not having her by my side on my wedding day. She was family.

Through our engagement, Brindy grew tremendously. The more she was around us, the easier it was for her to see I was not leaving her. We tried to include her as much as possible, but it took time to get used to the change. Looking back, if she had never dealt with what she had harbored inside her for so long, she might not have been able to adjust at all.

During the wedding weekend, a few people told me they could see how I had rubbed off on Brindy and that her mannerisms were similar to mine. Up to this point, I still wondered if I was doing the right thing, whether I had helped her or made her life harder. It was encouraging to hear they had seen a change in her since she first visited the U.S. and that she exhibited an aura that reminded them of me.

At our rehearsal dinner, it turned out she wasn't as shy or as nervous as we thought she would be. She gave a speech!

She ended the speech by saying, "You are my sister, my mother, my father, my everything."

Tears streamed down my face.

I believed in her... That's all I did. I saw her potential and gave her the chance to realize her purpose and chase after it. I know I cannot do this for every orphan or neglected child in the world, but I can encourage those like Brindy to let go of the hatred in their hearts and try to understand how they can move forward. It's easier said than done, but our ministry is determined to bring to light the hope that lives deep within every neglected child around the world.

67

I stared at the clock, continuously praying God would get us through this. I literally watched every second pass while I listened to surgery next door.

Every now and then, someone checked on me. I was extremely uncomfortable, but I didn't say anything because I didn't want to take attention away from Daniel. My leg was still positioned on the wooden board from the ambulance and hadn't been adjusted in nine hours. My heel throbbed until I could no longer feel it.

While I listened to the slow chatter in Daniel's operating room, I watched the nurses come and go with supplies. I even saw them exchange the bucket of blood and gauze, which was frightening.

At one point, when a nurse darted out the door, her abrupt movements frightened me. A few minutes of commotion and all I could do was pray, so I did.

Things seemed under control, but that didn't make the clock tick faster.

An hour later, when the nurse examined me, I lied and said I was okay, but the noises in the other room terrified me. *Is he okay? Are we going to be okay?* No one could answer that question at this point.

Eventually, a nurse entered my room with a giant wad of green bed sheets. She carefully peeled back one layer at a time from what seemed like a never-ending bundle. Finally, she uncovered operating tools in preparation for my surgery. She didn't touch anything. The way the sheets unfolded kept everything sanitary, or at least it seemed that way, but it was definitely an odd method.

The doctors cleared out of Daniel's operating room. A nurse came and told me everything had gone as planned. I hoped he was okay.

For thirty minutes, I lay there waiting for my surgery. The doctors took a dinner break. I had watched 5,400 seconds tick by, and now it was my turn. The anesthesiologist walked in and sat beside me. He asked if I was ready. *Should I tell him how long I have been waiting?*

He explained how the anesthesia would make me feel. He then asked me to roll over and gave me a shot to numb the area. The next needle was the epidural. He said he gave me something else to help me relax during the surgery.

I did nod off a few times, but only for a few seconds. They put a curtain between my chest and my legs so I couldn't see anything, but I heard everything.

Finally, surgery was over and my leg was wrapped up. They rolled me into the recovery room so the nurse could make sure I was recovering well enough to go back to the other room. When I arrived in the new room, I looked around for Daniel. I didn't want to be alone anymore. I found another clock to stare at and started passing the time.

The nurse walked over and said she'd have to observe me for an hour. My tears erupted. I was so tired, and I had held everything in until then. I had to be strong and translate and take care of us, but at that point, I just wanted to be with my people. I couldn't breathe. The machine beeped loudly and I panicked. *Another hour!* I didn't think I could do it. It was all starting to hit me—the trauma.

The nurse said she'd let me go early if I remained calm. I took a deep breath and watched the seconds tick by.

About forty-five minutes later, she rolled me to the room where Daniel and I would spend the next several days. When I saw him and our friends, I couldn't hold back the tears. They were happy to see me and thought I would be happy to get there, but I just cried. I covered my face. I couldn't hold it together anymore. It had been twelve agonizing hours since the accident—the most stressful twelve hours of my life. The trauma was devastating.

For the next five hours, we weren't allowed to sit up until the epidural wore off. By the last hour, the pain in my back was excruciating. I wanted to stretch so badly to stop the cramping. I had been in the same position for almost twenty hours. Finally, the clock proved our time was up, and we sat up and experienced some relief.

68

Living with a white girl made me feel lucky sometimes, but other times I was embarrassed. People asked if I was her helper, and occasionally I would answer "yes" even though it was not true. However, because of her, I felt like a princess no matter what other people thought when they saw us together. She treated me like a real person and taught me right from wrong. She cooked for me and woke me up in the mornings when breakfast was ready. She bought things for me and even let me see her hometown in America. She shared her sadness and happiness, and we cried and laughed together. She picked me up from school sometimes and helped me wash my clothes and clean the house. She showed me what a true family was.

"Ate Nat" was getting older and needed a partner in life. I knew she had a long-distance boyfriend, and for ten months, they didn't see each other except through FaceTime. I didn't care if she had a boyfriend while we lived in Malaybalay because all her attention was still on me.

I met her boyfriend in 2013 when we went to America. It felt like nothing important at first, but as the days passed, he was always there, hanging out in the house. I cannot explain what happened in my heart because I don't understand why I got mad and began to hate him. He went everywhere with us. When I was mad at Natalie, I didn't talk to her. I knew that hurt her, but I couldn't control it.

I was nineteen at the time, and the first thing that came to my mind was what would happen to me if Natalie married? She was the only person I had. I struggled with my emotions, the culture, and the language.

I didn't expect to have a difficult time making Daniel my friend. I saw him every day. He took up a lot of Natalie's time, and I felt Natalie didn't care about me anymore. I tried to keep my emotions to myself, but sometimes I couldn't hide them. I'd go to my room and cry.

I thought Natalie was my weakness, and I believed many lies telling me she would leave me someday. I realized, after we talked to the counselor, that this was a pattern in my life—people always leaving me. That's why I didn't trust people.

When we got back to the Philippines, Daniel came with us to visit. He was our neighbor, so it was like living with a boy when I saw him every day. We were together buying groceries and watching movies, but I didn't go with them everywhere. Sometimes when I got home late, I'd lock my door and not talk to them, especially not to Natalie. It was worse than a nightmare. Every night I cried.

After one month, he returned to America, and I started school. We were back to our normal routine, just the two of us. After a few months, I found out Daniel was moving to the Philippines, and I didn't know how to face this emotional roller coaster again.

Always being angry with them affected my studies and my church attendance, so Natalie decided I needed to get my own place. A part of me was happy, but mostly I was sad. I transferred to another house and did not see her, talk to her, or text her. I didn't give Daniel a chance to be part of my life.

In December of 2014, they went home to the States for Christmas. It was painful I could not go with them and that the person who had brought me to this city was not here for Christmas, so I celebrated Christmas by myself.

I prayed God would change my life and my emotions toward Daniel in the new year, 2015. It was not easy to accept that the person who took care of me was starting a new part of her life. I heard she was getting married and was happy for her, but I cried and told myself I would not cry about it again.

My New Year's resolution was a promise that this was the end of being hurt and that I would change my life to try to give Daniel a chance to be like an older brother. Every day, I prayed God would protect my heart, my emotions, and my mind from every lie I heard. I began noticing God was answering that prayer and protecting my heart.

The only reason I didn't like Daniel was because I was scared Natalie would leave me and that I wouldn't be able to hang out with her again. I was scared I had lost her. I thought Daniel took my place.

Everything happens for a reason, and the reason makes me stronger. I realized my life doesn't revolve around Natalie. She has her own life, and I have mine. She needed a husband in the right time. It was the right time for her, but I didn't know that at the time.

I'm old enough to understand everything now. She's married, and they are happy. I understand she never left me, but I miss her and the memories we made. Life has difficulties, but Natalie's always been there to encourage me. I think she still loves me.

69

That season, Brindy grew and for the first time allowed herself to trust that I was not going to leave her. Though I had repeatedly communicated that to her, she struggled choosing whether to believe me or the lies in her head telling her she was not important.

During these times, I reminded her of our sessions with Rob, the counselor in the U.S. I cannot imagine how hard it must be to be told and learn to understand that what you have believed your entire life is actually a lie. It was a major development for her to discover that she was worth more than she believed, but it was not an easy fact for her to internalize.

Brindy made a breakthrough when she vowed 2015 would be the end of her struggle in believing the lies. Things did not change overnight, but she made a promise to herself and continually prayed for the strength to make that resolution a reality. That was a huge step toward the freedom that I longed to see in her and what Jesus longed to give her. She was the only one who could allow that freedom to take over.

As the year progressed, I saw huge differences in her attitude toward Daniel and her thankfulness in general. She matured so much and is now able to help others through similar situations.

Since the beginning of knowing Brindy, she expressed a desire to help other orphans like herself. Now that she has learned from her own experience, she is ready. Her degree in social work will equip and qualify her even more to make a tremendous difference in the Philippines and around the world with Ellipsis. Her testimony is powerful, and I know God will use her to help many break free from the bondage of their pasts.

70

The nurses checked our vitals every few hours and everything seemed to be going well. Later the next morning, we had a few visitors. The first was our neighbor, whom we had not yet met. She traveled a lot for work but heard about us and wanted to come and see us. She sat down, and we made small talk.

She said, "You do know who hit you, right?"

"No, he never got out of the car," I replied.

"He is actually one of our neighbors. He lives in the big yellow house just down the street. He's the one who has lots of men at his house all the time, drinking and gambling. He used to be the mayor of a city that is predominately Muslim, and he is a drug pusher, too. You should definitely make him pay for this, what he did to you."

I didn't know what to say, but I knew this was a lot worse than what was underneath the bandages around our legs.

Later that day, one of the board members of our organization traveled several hours to check on us and answer concerns we had after hearing from our neighbor. She met with the police as a representative for us, since we obviously could not be present.

Unfortunately, the interview with the investigator I had unofficially entered into in the emergency room was skewed against us. I had told her, "By the time the car turned in front of us, we were going too fast to stop." I explained further that if we had slammed on the brakes, we would have skid onto the concrete and possibly into the lane of oncoming traffic.

There hadn't been time to react—the accident just happened. All the investigator heard was "we were going too fast." That's not what I had said in context, and I have never once seen a speed limit sign in the Philippines. We were not going fast, but we were cruising at a speed that didn't give us time to stop when he turned.

The board member told us the driver sent a representative as well. Since he was high profile, he didn't want any part in the meeting. He had his representative say it was our fault and we needed to pay for the damage done to his car. A tiger mural was painted on the front hood of the driver's SUV, which had a giant dent in it from Daniel's helmet. His car had minor damage, but our moped was totaled and we didn't know if we would ever walk again.

"You can't go against this guy. He will win. He would probably pay you what you ask for, but then he would possibly kidnap you and get the money back and more," the board member told us. "This is a dangerous guy, and he could send people to get you and take you to trial in his town, and you would not win. It's not worth the danger. He is very bad, and you don't want him to be mad at you, especially with your ministry in town. You want him to stay away from that."

It was hard to let it go. We struggled in anger that someone could get away with this. It wasn't fair.

That day, we called our parents to let them hear our voices after surgery and give them an update. When we talked to my mom, she asked if we needed her to come and help. That's when I realized we would need help for a while. I couldn't keep Brindy from going to school, or Leah and Meagan from overseeing the ministry. We needed 24/7 help we didn't want to admit we needed, but I'm thankful I had the courage to say yes.

Mom was on a plane the next morning. She was supposed to land in Manila the following night and join us Monday morning in CDO. Brindy and Kitchie, one of our friends, stayed with us that night. The next day was Brindy's twenty-first birthday. We never intended to celebrate her birthday in the hospital, but my good friend Vicky brought barbeque ribs and chocolate cake from her restaurant so Brindy could at least blow out a candle.

That day, Daniel's pain level couldn't be controlled. The nurses didn't want to change anything until we saw the doctor, but he wasn't coming until the next day. Finally, they switched one medicine and added another. Not long after, he got a horrible headache. They couldn't give him any more pain medicine through his IV, but we asked if he could take some Advil. We had to send someone to the pharmacy in the next building and pay for it before they would give it to him. It helped a little, and he was so tired from the pain that he drifted off.

He jolted, looked at me, and asked how long he had been asleep.

"A few minutes," I said.

"I think I stopped breathing when I fell asleep," he said. "Can you make sure I'm breathing when I sleep?"

I struggled to stay awake myself, but I watched him fall asleep and sure enough, he stopped breathing. I shook his shoulder, and he gasped. *What was happening?*

He said the room felt as if it was closing in on him. "I can't breathe," he said.

I pushed the button to call the nurse, and we explained what was happening. She checked his vitals, and said, "Everything looks fine."

Thirty minutes later, he didn't feel any better and his headache was worsening. I called the nurse again. Same routine. "He is okay."

Not long after, I looked over, and Daniel was almost incoherent. He was tensing up with his chest high and his head back in a sort of convulsing motion. Something was not right.

This time when the nurse came in, I begged her to do something. "He is not okay. Something is wrong!" Tears welled. I didn't know how to make them realize they needed to do something instead of saying everything was okay and "The doctor will be here in the morning."

"Daniel can't wait until morning. You have to help him now. I think he's having a reaction to the mixture of pain medicines."

It only got worse. About this time, I received a text that my mom had landed at the airport in CDO and was in the car with Leah and Meagan on their way to the hospital. I didn't want to scare Mom before she arrived, but I asked them to hurry. I didn't know if Daniel was going to make it. Moreover, no one was helping.

I tried to hold it together because I didn't want Daniel to worry. I hadn't slept at all because I had to make sure he was breathing.

When Mom walked in, she came straight to me and embraced me. I let go at that moment, and tears poured uncontrollably.

"Mom, you have to do something. Daniel is not okay, and they won't listen. I can't..." I whispered while she hugged me.

She walked over to Daniel and realized immediately something wasn't right.

Before she arrived, I had made several phone calls to get the doctor's number to contact him myself. He was the next one to walk in.

Daniel did have a reaction to the medicine, but by the time the doctor arrived, the antidote wouldn't have done much. The reaction had started to wear off, and the doctor assured us they would not give those medicines again.

That was the first time we had seen the doctor since surgery, and it was comforting to have him there. It was time to change our bandages and see the damage.

Daniel was first. His staples formed a Mercedes-Benz symbol on his kneecap, which he thought was cool. He also had a three-inch gash on the side of his leg lined with more staples. His wounds looked a lot better than a few days previously. The doctor cleaned and re-bandaged them.

Then, it was my turn.

As the layers came off, I went back and forth in my mind. *I'm gonna look. I'm not looking… Okay, I'll look.*

And there it was, an eight-inch Frankenstein worm of skin stitched together perfectly in line with my shinbone. Based on the look on my mom's face, I could tell she was shocked at how seriously injured we had been. We had a long road ahead. Daniel's injury was messy, but mine was just ugly and hard to look at.

"How in the world did my leg get a giant, perfectly linear gash from hitting an SUV?" I said. No one had any idea what could have done that, especially since I had been thrown off the moped. I sustained immediate impact and injuries from my fall. It didn't make sense.

71

Sometimes there is a warning and sometimes events happen blindly. In 2013, a typhoon hit the Philippines. We stayed in a hotel because our house was in a flood zone, and our center was open for the kids to seek shelter. We were ready for that storm and afterward, we didn't see damage in our city. However, I couldn't help thinking about the storms we face daily... *What about those?*

That week we started our education program. We decided we had to take a leap of faith and go for it. We didn't know if the kids would be interested, but they loved it! We saw seventeen-year-olds coloring in coloring books, which was plenty of evidence God had called us to something special. We glimpsed what they had missed for many years and a vulnerability that allowed us to show them a love that only Jesus could provide, all the while equipping them with tools of reading and writing that would change their futures.

However, the biggest "storm" of all remained— Rugby or Vulcaseal—which was an ongoing battle. When we met the kids' needs, they no longer needed the mask the drugs created, but they were already addicted. It's a storm, a long-lasting issue that is suffocating at times.

But if you can swim, *you swim.*

You don't give up until it's over or God takes you first. We would not give up. Whatever it took to teach those precious children about life and the Lord was worth every headache.

Every day, we saw great strides of progress, but we also saw regress. With any change, there's a journey. Just as one tries to break a habit, he may often fall back into it until he completely breaks free.

72

My whole body hurt... my legs, my knees, my arms, and my heart from restraining one of my favorite little boys who was too high to calm down and stop fighting. JJ was eleven.

This particular day, we arrived at the center and found pure chaos. The fight started in Divisoria, the city square where our kids hung out, and because it was school time, they brought the fight to us. Unfortunately, they got there before we did and caused a lot of commotion outside our center, luring all neighboring business owners to come out and watch or lock their doors in fright.

When street kids fight, they don't just hit one another. They find things to throw or use to really hurt one another. One of the main reasons they went to those extremes was Rugby, the drug. Addiction kills and it was killing these kids from the inside out. The kids were not themselves when they were high.

Everyone—other kids, the landlord, the neighbors— worked to calm down the kids and find out the problem amidst the chaos. I walked toward my little man, JJ, and he flailed out of control. I had never seen him like that. He yelled at me, calling me the worst word there was in Visayan. At that point, I still had no idea what was wrong with him or what had happened.

He then said he wanted to go home. I agreed that was a good idea and let him go, but I followed him. The first thing he did was grab an enormous rock to throw at the staff and me. We convinced him to put down the rock and tried to get him to come back inside. He found more rocks. It then became a chase. We couldn't leave him alone because he was angry, even throwing rocks at cars, but he ran away.

He returned. He came inside and tried to act normally, but that didn't last long. He became angry again. We couldn't let him go outside for fear he would throw rocks again. After a while, I decided to give him another chance to go home. This time he went for my car with the rocks. Finally, a bystander came to help, unlike the many others who stood watching.

Then we had to do something I had hoped we would never have to do. We had to let the police take him. He wouldn't calm down, and he wouldn't go home. He was high and angry. It broke my heart, but there was nothing more we could do.

That day, he wasn't himself—he was on Rugby. The police took him to the station to calm him down and had his dad pick him up so that he wouldn't get into more trouble.

We lived in an unfortunate reality. In street kid ministry, these kinds of battles were inevitable, but that didn't make it easy. We loved our kids, and we wanted to see them succeed. Every day, we got closer. Sometimes that addiction crept back in and got the best of them. Still, we held on to hope for JJ.

Through this experience, we noticed the need became greater for more to be done. These children needed not only a home and an education, but to be set free from the influences of the street and the trauma of their pasts.

We have since created a program called Freedom Camp, as well as an aftercare program, enabling children to begin the process of healing through the power of the Gospel and the help of counselors and psychologists. We believe progress is slowed down severely by trauma and, therefore, desire to enrich existing ministries and organizations with the tools to ensure their children have a chance to break free from the bondage of their past.

We know each child will have a different story and a different outcome and that healing does not happen overnight, but we believe our programs allow children the opportunity to move in the direction of healing in order to pursue their God-given purpose.

73

After the accident, Brindy had been sleeping on a tiny bench in the windowsill in the hospital. That first night of Mom's arrival, she gave Brindy a break from staying with us.

Every few hours, the nurses checked our vitals and gave us pain medicine. Four more times the nurses tried to give Daniel the medicine he had reacted to, so every time they came in, we had to ask what they were giving us to make sure it was the right medicine.

In the middle of the night, a new nurse walked in abruptly to take our vitals. He accidentally turned on the brightest light and then knocked over a giant water bottle near Daniel's bed.

The next morning, my mom got up to give Daniel his crutches to go to the restroom and noticed her pants around her ankles were wet. She looked around and found a giant puddle from the spilled water bottle the nurse hadn't cleaned up. If Daniel had slipped on that, he would have had another surgery. We were so upset.

I know my expectations were higher than they should have been. I'm sure the nurses were doing their best in the circumstances, but their normal is different from my experiences in the U.S. It was difficult for us to know what to expect or what we ourselves were responsible for.

Later that day, we were permitted to take sponge baths. The hospital only had one towel. Apparently, we were supposed to bring our own. We hadn't planned to be in the hospital, so we didn't pack a bag. We had to request plastic chairs for the shower as well. While we waited on the necessary shower supplies, an all-too-familiar Filipino gecko scurried across the wall. My mom was horrified—I wasn't shocked.

That night, it rained, and it wasn't long before the window bed Mom slept in was wet from the leaking windowsill. She had to use our shower towel to try to stop the rain from soaking her bed. Several hours later, a trail of ants scurried in from the rain and headed straight to our fruit stash.

That was it. We had had enough. We had only seen the doctor twice in the five days we healed in the hospital. Exhausted from caring for ourselves, we knew we'd be better off at home, and we got the green light to leave.

We loaded in the car the best we could. Daniel had to keep his knee from bending, so he stretched out on the back seat. I could bend my knee, but every time I went from horizontal to vertical, I almost passed out in pain. Getting blood flow to my foot was the strangest feeling, a pain that made even the numb areas around my wound react. Once my blood flow balanced out, I was okay for a little while.

On our way home, we passed the site of the accident and chills ran down my spine. Entering the gate was worse. Two blocks from our house sat the SUV, the dented lion's face on the hood. It was as if we were passing by in slow motion, and I had to relive the accident in that moment, still unsure how my leg had been split open.

Shaken up by how close we lived to the guy who had abruptly changed our lives, we pulled into the driveway and tried our best to get inside. This wasn't how I had wanted to show my mom our new house for the first time.

Our neighbors came out to say hello and ask if they could help, and it felt like we finally knew each other. I tried to say hello to my German Shepherd, but I couldn't get too close or he might knock me over. The poor thing was confused.

We sat on our brand new recliner couch and turned on the TV that had finally been connected the week before. We had nothing to eat. Home delivery didn't exist, so someone had to go to the store. Mom was the only one who could drive, but she had no idea where to go. I could use some exercise, so I agreed to go with her for the necessary groceries, medicine, and cleaning supplies. This was her first time to drive in the Philippines, which was a challenge.

Once again, we passed by the SUV that had hurt us so badly. Several other cars were there, and we wondered if he knew we were home. *Was he mad? Should we be worried?* There was an eerie feeling when we passed his home.

I was nervous walking around the mall. I had no idea what the guy who hit us looked like. He could be anywhere, and I didn't want to run into him, especially without knowing it.

While we were checking out at the grocery store, someone came up to me and asked if I was the one who was in the accident a few days previously. I affirmed, and he showed me pictures his daughter had taken of the accident. I couldn't believe I was alive after seeing them. I asked him to send them to me so I could have evidence.

He asked a familiar question: "You know who hit you, right?"

I nodded. I said the name.

"You need to make them pay. They have lots of money, and it's not right for them to get away with this," he responded.

We found out from the police report that the driver gave a pseudo name, the name of his right-hand man.

This wasn't a battle we could win.

After paying for the groceries and first aid supplies, I paid my phone bill. We were pretty sure we would be going home to America to finish healing and didn't need bills to pile up.

When we got home, Mom made dinner. We were exhausted. I had overdone it by "crutching" around the mall for too long. That had been my first time using crutches, and my arms ached from using them the wrong way. I had bruises to prove it.

I slowly headed to the stairs, but I couldn't do it. I could not go up one step. I turned, sat, and burst into tears. Mom hugged and cried with me. *Why? Lord, why did You let this happen?*

After a few minutes, Daniel suggested I go up the stairs backwards, using my arms to push up from stair to stair, which I did. Daniel came up, too, and we settled in bed for our first night back home. Afraid of kicking each other's legs in the night, we set up a pillow barrier and tried to relax. I couldn't. Tears flowed.

"He's right there," I pointed. "He could be drunk and come over and do whatever he wanted with us this close to him now."

I was overcome with fear when I realized how helpless we were. I could not heal in that environment.

74

Before one of my trips home, I created a testimonial video about our ministry to show supporters. I interviewed several of the kids, asking them to share how Streetlight helped them. A few had great stories.

Jo grew up in a well-off family. He had several siblings and seemed set for a successful life. One day, his parents began fighting, and it escalated quickly. Jo ran away. His mother abandoned his father and her children to start a new family, leaving the children feeling neglected and unloved.

One day, Jo decided he wanted to kill himself.

"Pero, ang pisi naputol!" He explained the suicide rope broke that day.

Before Jo joined Streetlight, he couldn't read or write. He was too ashamed to go back to school at seventeen, and he had no way to pay for it.

Though most schools are free in the Philippines, many of them require uniforms, materials for school projects in order to pass, and other hidden fees that force a child to choose between food on the table or an education. Small expenses make or break the chance of opportunity for a struggling family in the Philippines.

Streetlight was the perfect place for Jo because at his age and education level, he needed an alternative learning program that fit his needs. We collaborated with the local Department of Education to formulate a program where kids like Jo could benefit and be accredited with a legitimate education certificate. Today, he can read, write, and knows who Jesus is.

Alden was another boy who came through Streetlight with yet another incredible story. I video-interviewed him telling his story the same day as Jo.

After the interview, I was compelled to talk with him. He came from a Muslim family who had certain goals for his life that he didn't agree with. He ran away to find himself, and he found us.

That day after I turned off the camera, I asked him if he truly knew what he believed. He had been around Streetlight, and it was evident our programs encompassed Christian values. He admitted he had never felt so loved. He said he knew and believed Jesus was real and true. I didn't know how significant that conversation and that day would become.

It was incredible to watch these children change, to see them go from survivors to thriving children. It was beautiful to see anger, pain, and sadness turn into joy, laughter, and fun. There was nothing like it, and I can't imagine it ever getting old.

We literally witnessed miracles daily, because every day curve balls were thrown at us. Every day we faced impossible challenges, but God gave us strength. We prayed and sought Him through it all because prayer was our best weapon and, at times, the only weapon. There were times when I tried to take matters into my own hands, but I knew that would get me nowhere fast. God truly taught me to trust Him with the big and the small.

This wasn't a ministry that succeeded by force. Our approach was love. When family, friends, drugs, and false gods failed them, God's love remained. The greatest joy was seeing love become the medium that introduced them to Christ. *Would you trust a family that has forsaken your desires and forced you to follow their god when Abba Father stands beside you and will carry you through whatever you face?*

It must be difficult to see past one's family in order to know Christ if the members oppose Him. Family is usually the first thing we believe in because it is all we know growing up. What strength Alden showed in realizing something wasn't right when he left in search of answers. Though the answers caused him pain because he disobeyed the ways of his heritage, he will have an eternal destiny full of that love he experienced at Streetlight.

Later that night, I watched while tears rolled down Alden's face when he realized he didn't have to change or follow rules for God to love him unconditionally. He saw that love for several months, which changed his life forever. Right there in Divisoria, he stood up for himself and didn't do what he was "supposed" to do based on his family religion. He said he had decided to trust Jesus.

Jesus Christ gives us a choice to follow Him. There's nothing you have to do or even can do to get to Heaven. From Alden's reaction that night, I believe this young boy was beginning to realize who the true God was. His name is Yahweh.

Those are the moments, and that's the purpose of what we do at Ellipsis. Yes, we started by taking care of street kids and repairing their families. But most of all, we show them a love that will never fail them—a love that is eternal in Christ Jesus.

That was the last night we saw Alden. His family found him. I am thankful they cared enough to search for him. The real reason for his running away was to find Jesus, and I pray he never forgets his way. One day, maybe he will be the light among his family and neighborhood, pointing them toward Jesus.

75

"The thief comes to steal, kill and destroy, but I have come to give you life abundantly" (John 10:10).

I went into a meeting thinking it was about finding men to help with our ministry when the thief attacked. Everything I had moved to the Philippines for and lived for was threatened, beaten down, and crushed to my very core. Imagine everything you're living for trampled by three people.

The local barangay captain, who was basically a community leader working under the mayor, invited me to a meeting through a letter that stated nothing about its purpose. I had been meaning to set up a meeting with the captain anyway, so I assumed this was merely an introduction meeting, welcoming a new program to the community.

When I arrived, I discovered two other people had been invited to the meeting as well. One I recognized as the landlord of our ministry center. The other attendee, I soon found out, was the owner of the business across the street from our center. I had been invited to a meeting requested by those local business owners about our presence in their neighborhood.

They were angry our ministry center had brought street kids to their area. They only saw the negative side that they had to "deal with." Instead of asking us to talk with our kids about hanging around before or after our center was open, they told me everything they thought we were doing wrong. Their suggestions were incomplete, and my explanations were not heard. The meeting developed into an attack on our ministry instead of a step toward solving a problem. Our goal was to buy land and move outside the city, but it was a process and one we hadn't yet achieved.

I fought hard for the kids in our ministry and shared from my heart our purposes, plans, and stories about their growth, but nothing could penetrate the hearts of these leaders in the meeting.

We had to be willing to stand by our kids while they moved toward a better future. The process can be ugly and people can be negatively affected by it, but there is always a solution when people work together. In this situation, the local business owners were not willing to be affected for a short while for what we explained was the greater good of both parties.

Street kids are around every corner in CDO. These business owners couldn't claim street kids had never hung around their street. Imagine if we could team up with local businesses and gain their support to help more kids. We could eventually minimize or eliminate the number of street kids by giving them a home and an education. Community involvement was one of our top goals, but this particular group was not onboard with that idea.

But God, who is in us, is not beatable but has already been victorious!

Along the way, I knew there'd be trials to overcome, but I never expected such harsh backlash. The Filipino people are kind and loving at heart; therefore, I assumed through conflict that we would find resolution in a civil manner.

We continued praying more than ever that God would bring something good from our hard work. Jesus cared for "the least of these!" We planned to do the same.

76

After our first night home from the hospital, we sent Mom and my friend Vicky to see the city and different areas where we had been ministering. I didn't know when Mom would be back, and I didn't want to miss an opportunity to show her everything we had been doing.

When they returned, we talked about how Vicky could help us keep things going while we were gone. By that time, we had made a decision to go to Manila to see another doctor and start physical therapy until we could get back to America. We had several locals advise us it would be best if we left for our safety as well. I was grateful to have someone like Vicky, who was willing to go way beyond and help oversee what God had called us to do even while we were away. We didn't want the ministry to suffer because we had to leave.

That night, we packed everything that meant something to us and that we couldn't live without. We didn't know how this would play out and if we'd ever be back. Brindy helped us pack and spent time with us before we left. She was sad we had to leave and that we were unable to tell her when we would be back. It broke my heart not knowing our future and whether the Philippines would be part of it.

One of our other neighbors, a local radio host, arranged for a van to take us to the airport the next morning.

We left. It was an extremely emotional drive—still with no answers.

We reached Manila and stayed in a hotel near the nicest hospital in the city. We saw a doctor famous for treating professional athletes and Filipino Olympians, and it made us feel better to know our exact injuries and our expected recovery time.

77

A mother's worst nightmare happened on August 28, 2015. My phone was on silent from an event I had attended the previous evening, and I missed the call. Joe's phone rang, and immediately I knew something was wrong. I found my phone and listened to the voicemail Natalie had left. She was trying to be strong, but I heard the fear in her voice.

Joe and I sat in bed, and I grabbed my Bible while he dialed Daniel's parents and our pastor. We needed support and prayer.

After a long, fearful night, I made plans to leave on the next flight to the Philippines. The Lord was with me. He gave me strength and peace while traveling, and I trusted Him that our kids would be okay. We had prayers lifted up from friends all over the world, and we felt them.

Once I arrived, I realized how much they needed my help. It was unbelievable. I knew the situation was bad, but I was shocked at what I saw, from their injuries to the hospital conditions, and I wanted to get them home.

After the horror of spending time in the hospital and seeing the need to seek further medical attention, we decided to leave for Manila. I was told Natalie and Daniel were in danger staying in CDO and what could happen to them if we didn't leave. I didn't share in detail what I had been told, and I didn't sleep the two nights we were at their home. I felt we must leave as soon as possible and didn't want to scare them. I was there alone with the two of them. Neither could walk a step. It was a helpless, frightening feeling.

Once we booked our flights, we packed within a few hours, trying to grab anything of value they would need. Brindy came to help because Natalie and Daniel could not do anything at all, so we did the best we could.

The morning our ride came to take us to the airport, my heart was heavy. I sat in the front seat so Natalie and Daniel had room to prop up their legs. When we left the neighborhood and passed where the accident happened, tears rolled down my face. I knew they would never be able to return to their home. I knew their life as they knew it would never be the same.

Little children played in the street and precious Filipino people worked in the fields. These people needed their ministry. This all seemed so unfair. I cried because Natalie and Daniel were following the Lord's plan He had for them, and they didn't understand what was going on. I also didn't know what Brindy thought, leaving her behind. I prayed for God to be with us. We needed Him more than ever.

78

The fact that the term "street kid" exists is sad and wrong. I'm sure most would agree all children deserve a home and the street should never be an answer. However, this remains a reality for many.

One of our girls, Di, was going through a tough situation. She was eleven, the oldest girl of five children. Her mom collected trash for a living. Di had been collecting trash with her mom since she was a baby and had been exposed to "street life" through this experience.

In fact, there was an entire group of people so poverty-stricken that the only way they survived was by sifting through public dumping sites to collect resources to sell and food to eat.

Many times when a mother, or a father, is collecting trash, she will drop off her kids in Divisoria, the city plaza, and pick them up several hours later to go home. The kids meet other kids, and they learn some of the older kids never go home for different reasons, igniting a curiosity in the younger ones. They don't have the ability to understand why it's not safe because they haven't yet been exposed to the dangers.

Typically, one day, something happens: Mom comes around to gather her kids, usually in the middle of the night, and she can't find them. She searches and searches, but then goes home. *She goes home without them!*

I can guess what's going through your head right now. *How could you? How could you go home without them, much less sleep?* The answer is—*I have no idea.* My educated estimation is that this has been happening for generations and to them it's somewhat normal.

That first night, the child is introduced to the freedom of the street and all it offers. He or she soon feels invincible and free, without a care in the world. Friends pass around a plastic bag containing a gray substance. They sniff it and pass it to Di. She does it, too. At first, it's weird, and she doesn't like it. But later on or even the next day, she's hungry or scared, and she sniffs it again, the glue.

This glue, called Rugby or Vulcaseal, releases addictive vapors. It makes Di feel better, and she's hooked. Her friends are doing it, and it eases her pain. She sees no reason not to sniff it.

"I don't want to go home because they make me clean the house," Ami once said. She became a street kid the same way as Di had and didn't want to go home because freedom was more desirable than the rules of home.

This is the story of most of the kids we met and how many of them are introduced to the streets and to drugs. A lot of them have families and homes, and they can go home. They even do sometimes, but it's not enough. A roof can't keep them fed or safe in every situation.

The drop-in center called Streetlight was the first step of our ministry. We provided food, showers, school, Bible study, and a place to play. It took time and was a process to get a kid completely off the street.

Meo, the boy who broke his leg, was the first to be off drugs and off the street. He proved this process can work, but it's tough.

Di used to go home at night. One day, she didn't go home for several nights in a row. When she returned, her dad was angry and beat her. This happened a few times before she decided not to return. She stayed with her friends, and then her mom arranged for her to stay with an uncle. One day, we found out she wasn't going to her uncle's but sleeping on the street—alone, at eleven years old.

We chose her as our first girl to try to remove her from the street and get off drugs. As expected, it proved to be difficult, but we committed long ago to never give up on what we'd been called to do. She obviously struggled through it and didn't know what to do with structure.

The first night she did great. She was excited to sleep at the center and called it home. The second night, when her best friend showed up after being gone for a few weeks, they disappeared. We found Di later that evening and talked with her about running away. She said she wanted to be with her friends.

I like to think of this ministry as a journey through a mountain range because there are so many ups and downs. We couldn't force Di to change. All we could do was give her a chance to choose to change. Hopefully, she learned it was up to her to choose her path.

79

I wrote a message to my friends back in America to give them an update so they could pray for us and know details that we couldn't share publicly, for safety purposes.

Hey, friends!

Daniel and I are doing ok. Still have a lot of recovering to do! We saw a doctor Friday who seemed positive and said we will try to take our stitches and staples out Wednesday. We are in Manila with better healthcare! We still need prayer against infection, and my leg is still swollen so that worries us. Seems like my leg is taking longer to heal than Daniel's. My cut was extremely deep. Please pray my leg will heal quickly so we can come home for rehab, physical therapy and just an emotional break!

We cannot post any information because we need to keep our whereabouts and plans secret because the guy who hit us is a dangerous guy. He did not even get out of the car after he hit us. He will not pay for any of the damages or medical bills and believes we owe him for the damage to his car. We were driving straight, and he was turning left into the gate of our subdivision. He stalled like he was going to wait until we passed. Then, he just went anyway, and we were too close by that time to avoid him. It was basically a head-on collision.

The car hit our left legs—that's where the damage came from. I flew ten feet in the air and landed rolling, thankfully. We are thankful no major arteries were hit because we didn't see a doctor for three hours. God spared us for sure!

We have been advised that it is not safe for us to be in CDO right now because the police are even afraid to go up against these guys. So, we are coming home as soon as possible to recover. The guy lives four houses down from our house; therefore, we didn't even feel safe to be at home until things cool down. This group of guys acts in extremes when they feel they are being unfairly accused of something... It's so twisted. This is obviously extremely difficult for us as we feel we are being ripped from our ministry right now. I know God has a plan, and we are seeking His peace and understanding as we recover.

Please do not post about any of our plans and if you tell anyone please say the same. I wanted y'all to know so you can pray. Don't even post that we are coming home. We don't want them to know anything.

Thank you for praying. You have no idea how much that means to us. This is so hard... more than just physically but spiritually and emotionally as well.

Love you all!

80

After two years of running the drop-in center, buying land, and building homes, it was tough to comprehend that our kids were still street kids in a literal sense, meaning they were not yet able to move into the homes we were building. So much had changed. They'd improved drastically, but it was easy to think nothing had changed, simply because they were not yet housed. Since we knew we wouldn't have buildings and homes for these kids for a while, we prayed for something that could make the drop-in center phase better.

Our entire team began an active search for a new, bigger, and more effective drop-in center, and God answered that prayer. Our old center was small, dirty, loud, hot, and surrounded by businesses that were not supportive. Within days, one of our teachers found a place we were interested in seeing. We made an impromptu visit to check out the new option. After seeing many other places, we knew this was it! It was a house, similar to a condo, with two floors, a kitchen, a room for a classroom, a living room, a dining area, and two bedrooms. To top it off, there was a basketball hoop in the back made from an old coconut tree trunk.

Compared to our old center, this was a total upgrade. To add to the blessing, the rent was cheaper per month by $65. That savings paid for half of one of our new houseparent's monthly salary. Living expenses and wages are much lower in the Philippines so every amount helps, and dollars go a long way. This new center allowed us to start the process of getting kids off the street one by one. Slowly, we offered those who had quit using drugs a chance to stay in the center.

Since day one, it has been our desire to raise awareness in the community of Cagayan De Oro, to bring them together to help us make their community a better place. We've begun to see people in the community change their view of street kids and come forward to help. For example, I joined a Zumba class, and my class came together and performed a "Zumba Party for a Cause," raising money for our ministry. Their event allowed us to furnish our new drop-in center. Looking forward, we know CDO will come together to help their own children.

81

We battled over the perfect and safest time to travel back to the U.S. We were warned that after major surgery, blood clots might form when flying, so we were afraid to leave too soon. For three weeks, we lived in a hotel room across the street from the hospital. A few times, we went out to do things, but it was always extremely difficult to get around in such pain and in the extreme heat.

We brought Brindy up to Manila to spend more time with her before we left. The first night she stayed with us, I had an anxiety attack. I couldn't breathe. Every time I closed my eyes, the accident replayed. However, many times I saw a different ending—one much more tragic. To have our legs ripped out from under us, our strength and our plan seemed completely defeated. *What was the point to this? How was this a part of God's plan?* I couldn't see it turning out for the good.

These anxiety attacks were frequent over the next few months, and I quickly realized PTSD is a real thing as I experienced it for myself.

We started physical therapy in Manila, which showed us how long the road ahead would be. Not using my leg for two weeks created a hurdle to overcome.

82

As the husband, *how could I let this happen?* After the initial shock of the accident, Natalie and I had a lot of time to think, and the more I thought, the more anger took a seat in the chair of my heart. I was mad for several reasons and at several people. I was mad at myself. I'm supposed to protect my wife from anything that could cause her harm. I felt I was doing a terrible job of that while we lay on the concrete, near a bike under a truck bent "ten ways to Tuesday." *Was this my fault? Should we have been on a scooter in the first place?* We could have easily lost our lives that day.

Thinking back to how the accident played out, my anger increased toward the SUV driver. I'm pretty sure most of us would have immediately jumped out of the car to see if the other party involved was okay. This guy didn't, which I thought odd at the time. Of course, we would come to learn he had a reputation of being involved in drugs and kidnapping and wasn't the most honest guy.

Instead of giving his real name to the police, he gave another name. He didn't want to take the fall! As if that wasn't enough, according to him the accident was our fault, and he wanted us to pay for his car damage. After the wreck, we were ten feet off the right side of the road. We most certainly were not driving in his lane.

Over the next few months, every time I thought about him, I burned with anger and didn't have the ability to forgive him. I've always had a natural inclination to take matters into my own hands, so there was a small part of me that wanted to go to his house and give him the "what for," but that's unacceptable, especially as a Jesus follower.

The anger grew to a nasty head one day while I was home by myself. I cried out to God in anger toward this man who didn't care he'd altered our lives. Except for a dent on his hood, he hadn't been affected. (The dent was pretty big, I might add!) I was confused why God would let this happen.

My anger started to be geared toward God, too. I finally got on my face and said, "Lord, give me a word. I can't hold onto this anymore." After another hour of sitting and crying, I opened my Bible. I found Ephesians 4:31 and 32, which says: "Get rid of all bitterness, rage and anger, brawling and slander, along with every form of malice. Be kind and compassionate to one another, forgiving each other, just as in Christ God forgave you." This was one of those moments in life when you laugh at how blatantly obvious God has to be, almost as if He's slapping you on the face, saying, "Do I have to paint a picture for you?"

After I read that, I forgave the man. It felt good. I could think about him without sinning, without wanting to curse him. It was a freeing moment in my healing process. I would be lying if I said there weren't times where I relapsed, but in that moment, I forgave him.

It's been a while since the wreck, and I don't have any grudges against him. God will make everything right eventually. I often imagine God bringing this story full circle. What if one day we have a chance to talk to this guy and, if he doesn't know Him already, he comes to know The Lord through this whole episode? That would be extremely cool. Our work in CDO, the Philippines, and Asia, I believe, is just getting started. The wreck seemed to try to stop us, but I believe it made us stronger to become prepared to do more.

83

Finally, we got the green light to fly home, and we were lucky enough to have bulkhead seats since Daniel couldn't bend his knee yet. We also needed to elevate our legs often.

We were so thankful to be home but still felt lost and confused. We secluded ourselves, cried a lot, and tried to take it one day at a time. We avoided crowds so we wouldn't have to relive the accident by answering questions. Though we knew people would only ask out of love, we were still not ready.

We needed to get out, so we traveled with my family every weekend to watch the University of Mississippi football games. It gave us something to think about besides the reality of what was suffocating us.

One weekend, we were in Oxford, Mississippi, for a game and attended church that Sunday for the first time in the U.S. since the accident. That weekend, the church was sending a couple, who had served on their staff, back to their home state of Washington, near Seattle. Someone mentioned to us that the pastor of their church in Seattle was in attendance, and we needed to meet him. We had always loved the Seattle area.

We introduced ourselves, and he asked the obvious question of why we were both on crutches. We gave him the five-minute version of the most chaotic six weeks of our lives. For the first time, someone responded with sincere concern for our inner healing by saying, "I can't imagine what you're going through, but I want to help you through it."

He was the first person to understand we weren't struggling so much with the physical pain as much as the emotional and spiritual pain. One minute we were living our lives in another country, helping street kids and serving the Lord, and the next we'd been brutally knocked down in what was spiritual warfare more than anything else.

He invited us to Seattle to get away, to try to clear our minds, and to begin healing within. Though healing truly began that day, remnants of August 28, 2015, will forever go with us. However, it changed us in ways we still see. We are stronger. We are wiser. We do not depend on our own strength to carry through with God's calling on our lives. As long as we are here, we will follow the Lord, knowing He is ultimately in control and never left us for a second on the road we've traveled.

84

I wrote a blog a few months after the accident to update everyone on what happened:

I imagined my first blog after the wedding would be about getting our life started together in the ministry, but that's not what was in store for us...

I am still in shock and have to blink twice when I realize we are in Mississippi. We were not expecting to be home for about a year after the wedding. God must have other plans for right now. We still do not know what all God is going to do through this, but we are praying daily and taking things one day at a time.

We have wondered and questioned every possible aspect of the accident and why it happened. We may never know... I have even thought back to the day and the events that took place before we left the house that Friday. There were many factors that caused us to leave at the exact moment we left, and that's the only thing that could have had us in the exact place at that exact time...

It was a holiday in CDO, and we were looking forward to being able to have an "extra Saturday"! Honestly, any minor detail could have kept us from the time and place of the accident. It's bizarre to think back on even the tiniest details... Daniel walked out the door with his backpack with his laptop in it. If he had left it, it wouldn't have been destroyed by the impact.

I am super thankful for the detail that we both put on our helmets before leaving! Not that that's unusual, but certainly not everyone in the Philippines wears a helmet. Actually, most people don't...

Our bike was totaled, Daniel's computer was ruined and our left legs endured deep lacerations and a muscle tear from the impact of the SUV that are continuing to heal. We are both doing physical therapy, and Daniel is waiting for an MRI to see if there is more damage to his knee than originally assumed. These scars will forever tell a story that has changed us and impacted our lives.

That moment and the days to follow still haunt me. If you've ever been in an accident, you know exactly what I'm talking about. This is a first for me. The emotional and spiritual trauma are lingering full force as we are healing physically daily.

Of course, there is so much more to share, and, in time, I will. But right now, we're searching for God's healing, His plan and His peace through this journey. And we ask that you continue praying with us. God has a plan! He always does.

Something I have noticed is that God has been with us every step of the way, even during the accident. I do cherish His presence as I reflect on the last month. His love and your prayers have completely covered us!

God did speak to me this weekend as we attended Oxford Community Church with my sister. Fish, the pastor, called the church to pray for one of their members in his battle with cancer. We prayed over his family. He is a husband, a father and a radiologist. I was overwhelmed with compassion for him as I cannot imagine what it must feel like to have helped so many walk through treatment and now he himself is facing this battle. I know he wonders why and is seeking God's plan through this as well.

I felt as if God revealed to me while praying for this family that one of the reasons Daniel and I may be experiencing something in our lives that doesn't make sense is because that happens to everyone, and God wants to use us to comfort and love one another as we face trials in life. I never would have been able to connect with people on this level without having experienced what we experienced and are experiencing... As it says in Romans 12:15, "Rejoice with those who rejoice; mourn with those who mourn."

In that moment, I was thankful, in a way, despite all of the pain and trauma we are experiencing. God is using every bit of this to teach us and mold us into becoming more like Him. For that, we cannot complain.

Again, thank you to all the prayer warriors out there. You helped save our lives!

85

Hey, Philippines Team!

We miss you all so much and cannot wait to see you. We are so thankful for each of you and how you have powered through tough times.

God has taught us so much and brought us through so much. After the accident, Daniel and I began searching and asking why. Of course, we are not always promised to know why things happen in this life, but we have continuously prayed that God would show us how He planned to use this for His good and glory.

We have always had a desire to do more one day and expand to help more kids in CDO, the Philippines, and around the world. We assumed this change and expansion would not happen for a few years, but God had different plans.

We are excited to announce that we are starting our own organization! Because we feel led to do more, we know we need to have our own organization to have the freedom to grow as God leads. All of you will be joining us, and not much should change except that things will hopefully be easier to manage because we are our own organization. We are so thankful for the ministry that has helped us get started, so that we would be able to branch out when we were ready.

There is a lot to do in order to set this up. We have a lot of paper work, etc. with the U.S. government. This will take up much of our time in the coming months. We will do everything in our power to keep things running smoothly as well as continuing to raise awareness about our ministry while we are in the U.S.

Please pray with us that we will receive approval to operate ASAP. God has big plans for our ministry, and we are so thankful to have you working and praying with us. We will be back and forth a lot more than usual to and from the U.S. because as the directors of this organization, we are responsible for the funding, operation, and sustainability of everything we do and have done.

I hope you will join in our excitement as we introduce Ellipsis to the world! That is the name of our new organization. An Ellipsis is the "..." (dot dot dot) that many place at the end of a sentence, meaning the sentence is not finished yet. I think you would agree that the story of our kids, and many kids like them, is not yet finished! God is not done with them. And Rugby or Vulcaseal is NOT their story. They are so much more than that, and we want to continue giving them and others the chance to choose to dream and achieve the purpose for which God created them.

We love each of you! We hope you know that and understand that God is doing something amazing. We must have faith in His way and trust that He is doing something through our ministry for eternity. Do not give up. Do not lose heart. Do not be discouraged. Through our tragedy of the accident, God is creating a miracle! And we pray you will see that unfolding as well. God is so good and so faithful to His children!

Please pray for this process!

Much love,
Natalie and Daniel

86

God created us to have a meaningful life, and He created us to serve Him and glorify His name. God created me to have a mission in this world to help orphans and neglected children. He allowed me to go through several trials in order for me to be strong enough to stand up to the struggles in my future.

Everything that surrounds me in my life is from Him. I let Him guide me, and He is the boss of my life. When I was at the orphanage, I realized that someday I wanted to help orphans just like me. That dream is now closer to reality because I will be leading Freedom Camps with Ellipsis, helping kids break free from the trauma of their past.

Not only do I want to help them through their trials, but I want to help them in their heartache by telling them, "You are not alone, and you are strong enough to face your trials."

I will let them know I am here to help them.

Now I understand… This is why God took my parents away—so I would grow up at the orphanage and He could prepare me to help many children. He never left me. I am not forgotten. I am treasured and so are the rest of the kids out there just like me.

EPILOGUE

Brindy is just one of millions who deserve to live their lives fully. Through our organization, we offer a possible solution to what many like her will face. There is hope. We can make a difference. They do have a chance because their story is not yet finished... We desire to keep a child's past from dictating the direction of his/her future.

We plan to see the lives of many more children across the world experience this transforming, healing power of the redemption and love that Brindy and the streets kids of Cagayan De Oro feel through our ministry. God has a greater plan for us, and He is calling us—together with your help—to reach these and other groups of children.

At Ellipsis International, we have put together a camp we plan to take to orphanages, street ministries, and communities around the world where kids are in need, encouraging neglected children to believe in themselves and find purpose through the power of the Gospel. The dirt on their body or the dirt in their past may place a label on them, but it doesn't need to define them nor finish their story...

Our camp is structured like other summer camps, with games, music, stories, and activities, but with the purpose of addressing suppressed issues in children and aiding them in coping and conquering those issues rather than being defined and inhibited by them. From what I have learned through the stories of *The Forgotten Ones,* like Brindy, these camps will serve to jumpstart a change in many kids' futures. All activities are centered on ideas and principles recommended by licensed counselors and psychologists to uncover suppressed issues.

By the end of the camp, we hope children will have addressed what has happened to them and begin their journey of healing. Our mission teams will also equip locals, orphanage houseparents, pastors, or community volunteers to oversee follow-up gatherings for kids to continue asking questions or to dig deeper and be discipled by someone they know. We know healing doesn't happen overnight, but we have to start somewhere and allow our aftercare program to continue the process once we're gone. Our dream is that the "Brindys" of the world will experience "freedom" as early as possible in their lives.

If you would like to be a part of one of these camps, mission trips, or bring a camp to your location, please contact us. We cannot do this alone. Help us encourage children to dream!

AFTERWORD

The accident may have altered our lives, but it ultimately made us stronger. Because of that, we were able to start Ellipsis International, a dream we thought was years down the road. We have met so many people along our journey who have encouraged us and become like family.

God has definitely tested our marriage, but we made it this far. We faced more in the first year of marriage than most people ever face. We learned to lean on God's provision when things are out of reach, which is most of the time. I believe He likes to work that way so we cannot claim credit for all He has done. People are often amazed by what we have done in our ministry in such a short time, and I am quick to correct them because we have done nothing ourselves.

God has performed a miracle in restoring Brindy's life as well. Through the ups and downs, I wasn't sure if she would make it. However, I felt an uplifting Spirit within me, encouraging that the day would come when she would experience freedom. She has a new life, a new purpose, and a hope that exudes from within her. Because we gave her a chance, she is no longer labeled as forgotten... She is loved and will never feel forgotten again.

CONTACT INFORMATION

Natalie's personal website:
www.nataliestephensherrington.com

Natalie's Facebook:
www.facebook.com/nataliestephensherrington

Natalie's email:
nataliestephensherrington@gmail.com

Natalie's Instagram and Twitter:
@natherrington

Ellipsis International's website:
www.ellipsisinternational.org

Ellipsis email:
ellipsis.us.info@gmail.com

Ellipsis Facebook:
facebook.com/ellipsisint

Ellipsis Instagram and Twitter:
@ellipsisinternational

Made in the USA
Lexington, KY
14 August 2017